DISCOVERING POETRY

A Poetry Course for Key Stage 3

DENISE SCOTT

ADAPTED BY SUE STEWART

Heinemann

Heinemann Educational Publishers
Halley Court, Jordan Hill, Oxford OX2 8EJ
A division of Reed Educational & Professional Publishing Ltd

OXFORD MELBOURNE AUCKLAND
JOHANNESBURG BLANTYRE GABORONE
IBADAN PORTSMOUTH (NH) USA CHICAGO

© Rigby Heinemann 1991
Adaptations © Sue Stewart 1993
First published 1991 by Heinemann Educational Australia.
This edition, adapted by Sue Stewart, first published by Heinemann Educational
1993.

02 01 00 99
10 9 8 7 6

ISBN 0 435 14042 6

British Library Cataloguing in Publication Data for this title
is available on request.

Designed by Luisa Laino, adapted and typeset by Design Revolution, Brighton
Holy Dan and Riley illustrated by Helen Holroyd
Cover design by Andrew Morrison
Printed by The Bath Press, Bath

CONTENTS

INTRODUCTION

In *Discovering Poetry*, students are asked to read, react and respond to a variety of quality poems chosen for their accessibility and their power to move or delight.

The react activities serve as a guided exploration of each poem or group of poems. Particular emphasis has been given to the sharing of ideas through discussion in pairs and small groups. In this way, it is hoped that students will come to realise that the appreciation of literature involves exploration and discovery, and that this is stimulated by an environment of shared ideas and understandings. Students can be referred to the group discussion guidelines below to help them nurture their small-group skills. Refer them, too, to the guidelines below for reading poetry aloud – a valuable and enjoyable activity.

After their initial explorations, students can choose from a series of response activities designed to extend their reactions to the poems, and to foster their own writing.

Chapters are arranged in ascending order of difficulty. While this in no way prevents the book from being used as a resource which you can dip into, it does allow it to be used as a complete and graded text for the first two years of secondary school. It should also be noted that Chapters 1 and 6, 2 and 7, 3 and 8, 4 and 9, 5 and 10 are companion chapters. The chapters in Part 2, therefore, may be used as extension work for the chapters in Part 1.

The glossary of poetic terms provides a simple, complete explanation of the poetic terms used in the text.

GROUP DISCUSSION GUIDELINES

- Listen carefully and critically to others.

- Be prepared to contribute to the discussion.

- Avoid interrupting others.

- Accept others' points of view.

- Recognise that everyone is entitled to an equal say.

- Stick to the subject, and encourage others to do the same.

- Avoid aggressive and dominant talk and behaviour.

- Be aware of the needs of other group members. A quiet or shy group member may need your encouragement to take part in the discussion.

- Keep the peace and avoid tension.

■ Realise that group discussion is a valuable language activity. You'll be learning how to listen, how to express yourself, and how to communicate effectively in a small group. You'll also further your understanding of the topic.

READING POETRY ALOUD

■ Do you find poetry reading difficult? There are three things to watch for during your initial reading:
– pause
– lines
– verses

■ Always pause at the various punctuation marks. Pause gives the poem its meaning and its feeling. So, look out for:
,   commas (short pauses)
.   full stops (longer pauses)
;   semi-colons (medium pauses)
...   dots (very long pauses)
–   dashes (long, climactic pauses)
!   exclamation marks (long, surprised pauses)
:   colons (medium pauses)

■ Most poetry is written in short *lines*. However, don't stop at the end of a line when reading unless there is a pause. Run the line on until the next pause.

■ Also, there may not be a pause between *verses*, even though there may be a space between verses. If there is no pause, run one verse into the other when reading.

■ Note any special feature of the poem that may need emphasising – for example, *alliteration* (see page 146) or *rhythm*.

■ Vary your *pace* and *volume* to suit the poem's meaning or atmosphere.

■ Use a suitable *tone* (see page 147) of voice to capture the poem's *mood* (see page 147).

■ Practise until you feel that your reading is as expressive as possible.

PLAYING WITH WORDS

READ

Poetic verse has always been the most popular form of communication to celebrate or commemorate life's special occasions. Poems written for a special occasion are called 'occasional poetry'. Here are just a few examples:

Birthday greetings to my friend.

Let our friendship never end.

I'm for you and you're for me,

Plain for anyone to see.

As fish swim
As doves coo
As birds fly
So I love you.
Please be mine,
Valentine!

Life may be brief
But memories are long.
From the heart of my grief
I'll still sing our song.

Death,
Like an ever-flowing stream,
Sweeps us away.
Our life's dream,
An empty tale,
A morning flower,
Cut down
And withered in an hour.

Safe in our hearts they will always stay.
Loved and remembered every day.

I'm sorry I said what I did,
I acted like a fool.
Please speak to me again
When I see you in school.

REACT

As a whole class, brainstorm a list of other instances in which poetry is used in everyday life – occasions, creations and publications (apart from poetry anthologies or similar) where it can be found.

RESPOND

Now make individual contributions to a whole class display of popular poetry. Include any occasional verse, any lines or expressions that you consider poetic. If you can justify that your choice is:

- original,
- artful,
- creative,
- rhythmical,

- beautiful or
- inspirational,

then you can probably call it poetic. Discuss what different class members judge to be poetry and what not. You should be able to explore some good ideas of what poetry is.

READ

There was a young lady from Niger
Who smiled as she rode on a tiger.
    They returned from the ride
    With the lady inside,
And the smile on the face of the tiger.

A painter who lived in Great Britain
Interrupted two girls with their knittin'.
    He said with a sigh,
    'That park bench – well I
Just painted it, right where you're sittin'.'

Said an envious erudite ermine:
'There's one thing I cannot determine;
    When a girl wears my coat
    She's a person of note:
When I wear it I'm only called vermin.'

A bow-legged policeman from Kew
Said: 'I really don't know what to do.
    I can stop without fuss
    A lorry or bus
But mini cars simply go through.'

There was a young girl of Australia
Who went to a dance as a dahlia.
    When the petals uncurled,
    It revealed to the world
That the dress, as a dress, was a failure!

A tutor who tooted a flute
Tried to teach two young tooters to toot.
    Said the two to the tutor,
    'Is it harder to toot, or
To tutor two tooters to toot?'

There was an old fellow named Green
Who grew so abnormally lean
    And flat and compressed
    That his back touched his chest,
And sideways he couldn't be seen.

3

REACT

As individuals, consider what is similar about all limericks – in their subject, topic, form or shape, and in their reason for being written. Using these similarities, try writing a definition of the word 'limerick'. Try to make your definition as concise as you can, whilst still including all the features you think are essential parts of a limerick.

RESPOND

1   As a whole class, try making up your own limericks. One person can start the ball rolling by calling out a first line: 'There was a ...'. This is written on the board. A second student then calls out the second line (which is also written on the board) and so on. Be spontaneous: just see what you can make in an unrestrained, creative spirit. (If the activity is really successful, you may need a second 'scribe' to record all the possibilities.)

or

2   Everybody in the class finds what they consider to be a particularly clever limerick. Collate all of these in a scrapbook or wall chart and vote for the best of the whole group. You could tally the results and add them in graph form to your scrapbook or wall chart.

4

Beau Peep

READ

Each of the limericks below depends on a clever word play.

There once was a pious young priest
Who lived almost entirely on yeast;
'For', he said, 'it is plain
We must all rise again,
And I want to get started, at least.'

The thunder god felt rather chilly,
So he went for a ride on his filly.
 'I'm Thor!' he cried,
 And the horse replied,
'You've forgotten your thaddle, you thilly!'

A lady there was from Antigua
Who remarked to her spouse, 'What a pigua!'
  He retorted, 'My Queen,
  Is it manners you mean?
Or do you refer to my figua?'

A fly and a flea in a flue
Were imprisoned, so what could they do?
  Said the fly, 'Let us flee!'
  'Let us fly!' said the flea,
So they flew through a flaw in the flue!

A major, with wonderful force,
Called out in Hyde Park for a horse.
  All the flowers looked round
  But no horse could be found;
So he just rhododendron, of course.

There once was a gnu in the zoo
Who tired of the same daily view.
  To seek a new sight
  He stole out one night,
And where he went gnobody gnu.

5

REACT

Each limerick uses a different kind of word trick. Together, they show how funny words can be.

In pairs, match each of the following statements with one of the limericks:

1   This limerick is based on the use of homophones (words like 'here' and 'hear' that sound the same but have different meanings).

2   This limerick is based on a pun (the humorous use of a word that can have more than one meaning).

3   This limerick is a tongue twister; it uses several words of very similar sound to create a humorous effect.

4   This limerick changes the spelling and shape of words to force them to rhyme with a preceding word.

5   This limerick is based on the deliberate misinterpretation of a word.

6   This limerick uses a suitably sounding word in a new and humorous way.

RESPOND

1　In your pairs, use one of the above kinds of word play to write your own
　　limerick.

　　or

2　Find at least one limerick that uses the same kind of word play as each of
　　the limericks above.

B.C.

READ

These little creations are both simple and crazy – or simply crazy! They were
written just for the pleasure of playing with words and sounds:

SMALL TALK

'Hello, Blue.'
'How are you?'
'I'm fine.'
'Me too.'

'How's Sue?'
'Nothing new,'
'How about you?'
'Not much to do.'

'What do you say?'
'I'm OK.'
'Want to play?'
'Not today.'

'Hello, Blue.'
'How are you?'
'I'm fine.'
'Me, too.'

DUNCAN BALL

ODE TO A GOLDFISH

O
Wet
Pet!

GYLES BRANDRETH

A WISP OF A WASP

I'm a wisp of a wasp with a worry,
I'm hiding somewhere in Surrey
I've just bit upon
The fat sit upon
Of the King – so I left in a hurry!

COLIN WEST

BAD REPORT — GOOD MANNERS

My daddy said, 'My son, my son,
This school report is bad.'
I said, 'I did my best I did,
My dad my dad my dad.'
'Explain, my son, my son,' he said.
'Why *bottom* of the class?'
'I stood aside, my dad my dad,
To let the others pass.'

SPIKE MILLIGAN

THE BIG BABOON

The Big Baboon is found upon
  The plains of Cariboo:
He goes about with nothing on
  (A shocking thing to do).

But if he dressed respectably
  And let his whiskers grow,
How like this Big Baboon would be
  To Mister So-and-so!

HILAIRE BELLOC

7

HAIR

I despair
About hair
   With all the fuss
   For us
Of snipping
And clipping,
   Of curling
   And twirling,
Of tying
And drying,
   And lopping
   And flopping,
And flurries
And worries,
   About strength
   The length,
As it nears
The ears
   Or shoulder.
   When you're older
It turns grey
Or goes away
   Or leaves a fuzz
   Hair does!

MAX FATCHEN

I wish I could run like a cheetah
and measure out a day.
Tomorrow would be just a metre,
an inch would be yesterday.

SUE STEWART

REACT

Decide which poem you think is:

- the silliest or most pointless; and
- the most unusual in content or idea.

As a whole class, compare and discuss your choices and the reasons for them.

RESPOND

1   Hold a class competition to find the cleverest simply crazy poem.
    or
2   Hold a class competition to create the cleverest simply crazy poem.

READ

Tall stories (stories that are highly exaggerated for humorous effect) are
often the subject of creative writing. See what you think of these.

FROM 'YARNS'

They have yarns
Of a skyscraper so tall they had to put hinges
   On the two top stories so to let the moon go by,
Of one corn crop in Missouri when the roots
   Went so deep and drew off so much water
     The Mississippi river bed that year was dry,
Of pancakes so thin they had only one side,

. . . .

Of a mountain railroad curve where the engineer in his cab
   can touch the caboose and spit in the conductor's
   eye,
Of the boy who climbed a cornstalk growing so fast he
   would have starved to death if they hadn't shot
   biscuits up to him,
Of the old man's whiskers:
   When the wind was with him his whiskers arrived a
     day before he did,'

. . . .

Of the sheep-counter who was fast and accurate: 'I just
   count their feet and divide by four,'
Of the man so tall he must climb a ladder to shave himself,

. . . .

Of the man who killed a snake by putting its tail in its
   mouth so it swallowed itself,
Of the railroad trains whizzing along so fast they reached
   the station before the whistle,

. . . .

CARL SANDBURG

AN EASY DECISION

I had finished my dinner
Gone for a walk
It was fine
Out and I started whistling

It wasn't long before

I met a
Man and his wife riding on
A pony with seven
Kids running along beside them

I said hello and
Went on
Pretty soon I met another
Couple
This time with nineteen
Kids and all of them
Riding on
A big smiling hippopotamus

I invited them home

KENNETH PATCHEN

CENTIPEDE'S SONG

'I've eaten many strange and scrumptious dishes in my time,
Like jellied gnats and dandyprats and earwigs cooked in slime,
And mice with rice – they're really nice
When roasted in their prime.
(But don't forget to sprinkle them with just a pinch of grime.)

'I've eaten fresh mudburgers by the greatest cooks there are,
And scrambled dregs and stinkbug's eggs and hornets stewed in tar,
And pails of snails and lizards' tails,
And beetles by the jar.
(A beetle is improved by just a splash of vinegar.)

'I often eat boiled slobbages. They're grand when served beside
Minced doodlebugs and curried slugs. And have you ever tried
Mosquitoes' toes and wampfish roes
Most delicately fried?
(The only trouble is they disagree with my inside.)

'I'm mad for crispy wasp-stings on a piece of buttered toast,
And pickled spines of porcupines. And then a gorgeous roast
Of dragon's flesh, well hung, not fresh –
It costs a pound at most,
(And comes to you in barrels if you order it by post.)

'I crave the tasty tentacles of octopi for tea
I like hot-dogs, I LOVE hot-frogs, and surely you'll agree
A plate of soil with engine oil's
A super recipe
(I hardly need to mention that it's practically free.)

'For dinner on my birthday shall I tell you what I chose:
Hot noodles made from poodles on a slice of garden hose –
And a rather smelly jelly
Made of armadillo's toes.
(The jelly is delicious, but you have to hold your nose.)

'Now comes,' *the Centipede declared*, 'the burden of my speech:
These foods are rare beyond compare – some are right out of reach;
But there's no doubt I'd go without
A million plates of each
For one small mite,
One tiny bite
Of this FANTASTIC PEACH!'

ROALD DAHL

11

REACT
'CENTIPEDE'S SONG'
This is a funny poem, and clever too: let's look at some of the poetic devices used. The poet's use of sound – rhyming words on the ends of the lines, rhyming words within lines (such as mice/rice/nice) and alliteration (see page 146) – makes the poem rollick along and helps to emphasise the nastiness of its 'delights'.

Look again at the first verse where some of these devices are highlighted for you:

CENTIPEDE'S SONG

'I've eaten many strange and scrumptious dishes in my <u>time</u>,
Like jellied <u>gnats</u> and dandy<u>prats</u> and earwigs cooked in <u>slime</u>,
And <u>mice</u> with <u>rice</u> – they're really <u>nice</u>
When roasted in their <u>prime</u>.
(But don't forget to sprinkle them with just a pinch of <u>grime</u>.)

Now copy out another verse from the poem and show how Roald Dahl has used rhymes and alliteration for 'sound effects'. What do they add to the poem?

'AN EASY DECISION'
In pairs, discuss the poem's title. Why do you think the decision was 'easy'?

YARNS
Make a collection of poems that some people would not accept as real poetry.

12

RESPOND

1 In pairs, prepare an expressive reading of 'Centipede's Song' (see reading guidelines on page v). Your performance should show that you recognise and appreciate the poet's use of rhyme and alliteration to create emphasis and effect. Check that you vary your:
   - pitch,
   - pauses,
   - pace and
   - volume

   to produce an expressive and entertaining reading.
   or

2 Look again at the form (see page 146) of 'An Easy Decision', then write an equally crazy little poem where you pay attention to its form.
   or

3 As a small group of four to six students, see how far you can get with yarns of your own. Use a form similar to the one used above.
   or

4 These poems might inspire some more crazy writing of your own – in prose or poetry. Wait until you're in the mood, then pen some unusual journal jottings.

TELLING STORIES

READ

'Legend' is a narrative poem, and tells us a fantastic story – or is it a tall tale?
See what you think.

LEGEND

The blacksmith's boy went out with a rifle
and a black dog running behind.
Cobwebs snatched at his feet,
rivers hindered him,
thorn-branches caught at his eyes to make him blind
and the sky turned into an unlucky opal,
but he didn't mind,
I can break branches, I can swim rivers, I can stare out any
    spider I meet,
said he to his dog and his rifle.

The blacksmith's boy went over the paddocks
with his old black hat on his head.
Mountains jumped in his way,
rocks rolled down on him,
and the old crow cried, 'You'll soon be dead.'
And the rain came down like mattocks.
But he only said
I can climb mountains, I can dodge rocks, I can shoot an old
   crow any day,
and he went on over the paddocks.

When he came to the end of the day the sun began falling.
Up came the night ready to swallow him,
like the barrel of a gun,
like an old black hat,
like a black dog hungry to follow him.
Then the pigeon, the magpie and the dove began wailing
and the grass lay down to pillow him.
His rifle broke, his hat blew away and his dog was gone
and the sun was falling.

But in front of the night the rainbow stood on the mountain,
just as his heart foretold.
He ran like a hare,
he climbed like a fox;
he caught it in his hands, the colours and the cold –
like a bar of ice, like the column of a fountain,
like a ring of gold.
The pigeon, the magpie and the dove flew up to stare,
and the grass stood up again on the mountain.

The blacksmith's boy hung the rainbow on his shoulder
instead of his broken gun.
Lizards ran out to see,
snakes made way for him,
and the rainbow shone as brightly as the sun.
All the world said, Nobody is braver, nobody is bolder,
nobody else has done
anything to equal it. He went home as bold as he could be
with the swinging rainbow on his shoulder.

JUDITH WRIGHT

REACT

In pairs:

1   Discuss the poem's rhyme. Look at the rhyme in the first stanza: behind/blind/mind, feet/meet, rifle/opal/rifle. Some of these rhymes are called 'near-rhyme' — can you see why? See if you can spot the rest.

2   Decide if you think the blacksmith's boy was a real person or not.

3   Discuss what you think the poem means, and what it's telling us about bravery.

Share your findings as a whole class.

RESPOND

1   Prepare a reading of 'Legend' (see reading guidelines on page v).
    or
2   Find a photograph or a character in a newspaper or magazine, and make up a legend or fantastic story about this character. Try to use a narrative form as close as you can to the form of 'Legend'.
    or
3   Find and read to the class another narrative poem about a character or situation which appeals to you.

READ

Characters and their life stories are often the subject of ballads, that is, narratives told in regular, rhyming, rhythmic stanzas (see ballad, page 146). Here are two ballads by Charles Causley, written about two very different people ... or are they? See what you think.

TIMOTHY WINTERS

Timothy Winters comes to school
With eyes as wide as a football pool,
Ears like bombs and teeth like splinters:
A blitz of a boy is Timothy Winters.

His belly is white, his neck is dark,
And his hair is an exclamation mark.
His clothes are enough to scare a crow
And through his britches the blue winds blow.

When teacher talks he won't hear a word
And he shoots down dead the arithmetic-bird,
He licks the patterns off his plate
And he's not even heard of the Welfare State.

Timothy Winters has bloody feet
And he lives in a house on Suez Street,
He sleeps in a sack on the kitchen floor
And they say there aren't boys like him any more.

Old Man Winters likes his beer
And his missus ran off with a bombardier,
Grandma sits in the grate with a gin
And Timothy's dosed with an aspirin.

The Welfare Worker lies awake
But the law's as tricky as a ten-foot snake,
So Timothy Winters drinks his cup
And slowly goes on growing up.

At Morning Prayers the master helves
For children less fortunate than ourselves,
And the loudest response in the room is when
Timothy Winters roars 'Amen!'

So come one angel, come on ten:
Timothy Winters says 'Amen
Amen amen amen amen.'
Timothy Winters, Lord.

Amen.

helves: a dialect word from north Cornwall used to describe the alarmed lowing of cattle (as when a cow is separated from her calf); a desperate, pleading note

CHARLES CAUSLEY

RILEY

Down in the water-meadows Riley
Spread his wash on the bramble-thorn,
Sat, one foot in the moving water,
Bare as the day that he was born.

Candid was his curling whisker,
Brown his body as an old tree-limb,
Blue his eye as the jay above him
Watching him watch the minjies swim.

Four stout sticks for walls had Riley,
His roof was a rusty piece of tin,
As snug in the lew of a Cornish hedgerow
He watched the seasons out and in.

He paid no rates, he paid no taxes,
His lamp was the moon hung in the tree.
Though many an ache and pain had Riley
He envied neither you nor me.

Many a friend from bush or burrow
To Riley's hand would run or fly,
And soft he'd sing and sweet he'd whistle
Whatever the weather in the sky.

Till one winter's morning Riley
From the meadow vanished clean.
Gone was the rusty tin, the timber,
As if old Riley had never been.

What strange secret had old Riley?
Where did he come from? Where did he go?
Why was his heart as light as summer?
Never know now, said the jay. *Never know.*

minjies: small minnows
lew: lee

CHARLES CAUSLEY

REACT

1 Do you think Timothy Winters and Riley are very different from one another? Or can you see similarities? Look, for instance, at verse 7 in 'Timothy Winters' and verse 4 in 'Riley'.

2 The two poems have very different tones or moods (see page 147). Can you describe the difference?

3 'Timothy Winters' is not just a story: it is beautifully written poetry. Find what you consider to be the poem's best examples of:
   * simile (comparison; see lines 2, 3 and 22; see also page 147)
   * metaphor (speaking about one thing as if it were something else; see lines 4 and 6; see also page 147)
   * visual imagery (a picture or image that we can clearly see in our minds because of the writer's clever use of words; consider verses 2, 3 and 4)
   * alliteration (repeated use of the same sound to create a special effect; see page 146).

RESPOND

1 Prepare an individual reading of 'Riley' (see reading guidelines on page v).
   or
   As a group, set 'Riley' to music; rehearse and present it to the class.
   or
   Imagine you met Riley before his disappearance. Then, in pairs, prepare an interview with him. Be sure to assume an appropriate character for Riley.
   or

2 Write your own story about a wise old person. It can be someone you know, or someone you invent.
   or
   Write at least three diary entries that Riley might have made at different times of the year.

19

READ

Australian bush songs and ballads introduce us to many unique and colourful characters who are usually the centre of a tall or unlikely story. Here, we meet Holy Dan, Mulga Bill and the man from Ironbark.

HOLY DAN

It was in the Queensland drought;
And over hill and dell,
No grass – the water far apart,
All dry and hot as hell.
The wretched bullock teams drew up
Beside a water-hole –
They'd struggled on through dust and drought
For days to reach this goal.
And though the water rendered forth
A rank, unholy stench,
The bullocks and the bullockies
Drank deep their thirst to quench.

Two of the drivers cursed and swore
As only drivers can.
The other one, named Daniel,
Best known as Holy Dan,
Admonished them and said it was
The Lord's all-wise decree;
And if they'd only watch and wait,
A change they'd quickly see.

'Twas strange that of Dan's bullocks
Not one had gone aloft,
But this, he said, was due to prayer
And supplication oft.
At last one died but Dan was calm,
He hardly seemed to care;
He knelt beside the bullock's corpse
And offered up a prayer.

'One bullock Thou has taken, Lord,
And so it seemeth best.
Thy will be done, but see my need
And spare to me the rest!'

A month went by. Dan's bullocks now
Were dying every day,
But still on each occasion would
The faithful fellow pray,
'Another Thou has taken, Lord,
And so it seemeth best.
Thy will be done, but see my need,
And spare to me the rest!'

And still they camped beside the hole,
And still it never rained,
And still Dan's bullocks died and died,
Till only one remained.
Then Dan broke down – good Holy Dan –
The man who never swore.
He knelt beside the latest corpse,
And here's the prayer he bore.

'That's nineteen Thou has taken, Lord,
And now You'll plainly see
You'd better take the bloody lot,
One's no damn good to me.'
The other riders laughed so much
They shook the sky around;
The lightning flashed, the thunder roared,
And Holy Dan was drowned.

TRADITIONAL

21

MULGA BILL'S BICYCLE

'Twas Mulga Bill, from Eaglehawk, that caught the cycling craze;
He turned away the good old horse that served him many days;
He dressed himself in cycling clothes, resplendent to be seen;
He hurried off to town and bought a shining new machine;
And as he wheeled it through the door, with air of lordly pride.
The grinning shop assistant said, 'Excuse me, can you ride?'

'See, here, young man,' said Mulga Bill, 'from Walgett to the sea,
From Conroy's Gap to Castlereagh, there's none can ride like me.
I'm good all round at everything, as everybody knows,
Although I'm not the one to talk – I *hate* a man that blows.
But riding is my special gift, my chiefest, sole delight;
Just ask a wild duck can it swim, a wild cat can it fight.
There's nothing walks or jumps or runs, on axle, hoof, or wheel,
But what I'll sit, while hide will hold and girths and straps are tight:
I'll ride this here two-wheeled concern right straight away at sight.'

'Twas Mulga Bill, from Eaglehawk, that sought his own abode,
That perched above the Dead Man's Creek, beside the mountain road.
He turned the cycle down the hill and mounted for the fray,
But ere he'd gone a dozen yards it bolted clean away.
It left the track, and through the trees, just like a silver streak,
It whistled down the awful slope, towards the Dead Man's Creek.
It shaved a stump by half an inch, it dodged a big white-box:
The very wallaroos in fright went scrambling up the rocks,
The wombats hiding in their caves dug deeper underground,
As Mulga Bill, as white as chalk, sat tight to every bound.
It struck a stone and gave a spring that cleared a fallen tree,
It raced beside a precipice as close as close could be;
And then as Mulga Bill let out one last despairing shriek
It made a leap of twenty feet into the Dead Man's Creek.

'Twas Mulga Bill, from Eaglehawk, that slowly swam ashore:
He said, 'I've had some narrer shaves and lively rides before;
I've rode a wild bull round a yard to win a five-pound bet,
But this was the most awful ride that I've encountered yet.
I'll give that two-wheeled outlaw best; it's shaken all me nerve
To feel it whistle through the air and plunge and buck and swerve.
It's safe at rest in Dead Man's Creek, we'll leave it lying still:
A horse's back is good enough henceforth for Mulga Bill.'

A. B. PATERSON

THE MAN FROM IRONBARK

It was the man from Ironbark who struck the Sydney town,
He wandered over street and park, he wandered up and down.
He loitered here, he loitered there, till he was like to drop,
Until at last in sheer despair he sought a barber's shop.
"Ere! shave my beard and whiskers off, I'll be a man of mark,
I'll go and do the Sydney toff up home in Ironbark.'

The barber man was small and flash, as barbers mostly are,
He wore a strike-your-fancy sash, he smoked a huge cigar:
He was a humorist of note and keen on repartee,
He laid the odds and kept a 'tote', whatever that may be.
And when he saw our friend arrive, he whispered, 'Here's a lark!
Just watch me catch him all alive, this man from Ironbark.'

There were some gilded youths that sat along the barber's wall,
Their eyes were dull, their heads were flat, they had no brains at all;
To them the barber passed the wink, his dexter eyelid shut.
'I'll make this bloomin' yokel think his bloomin' throat is cut.'
And as he soaped and rubbed it in he made a rude remark:
'I s'pose the flats is pretty green up there in Ironbark.'

A grunt was all reply he got; he shaved the bushman's chin,
Then made the water boiling hot and dipped the razor in.
He raised his hand, his brow grew black, he paused awhile to gloat,
Then slashed the red-hot razor-back across his victim's throat;
Upon the newly-shaven skin it made a livid mark –
No doubt it fairly took him in – the man from Ironbark.
He fetched a wild up-country yell might wake the dead to hear,
And though his throat, he knew full well, was cut from ear to ear
He struggled gamely to his feet, and faced the murderous foe.
'You've done for me! you dog, I'm beat! one hit before I go!
I only wish I had a knife, you blessed murdering shark!
But you'll remember all your life the man from Ironbark.'

He lifted up his hairy paw, with one tremendous clout
He landed on the barber's jaw, and knocked the barber out.
He set to work with tooth and nail, he made the place a wreck;
He grabbed the nearest gilded youth, and tried to break his neck.
And all the while his throat he held to save his vital spark.
And 'Murder! Bloody Murder!' yelled the man from Ironbark.

A peeler man who heard the din came in to see the show;
He tried to run the bushman in, but he refused to go.
And when at last the barber spoke, and said "Twas all in fun –
'Twas just a little harmless joke, a trifle overdone.'
'A joke!' he cried, 'By George, that's fine; a lively sort of lark;
I'd like to catch that murdering swine some night in Ironbark.'

And now while round the shearing-floor the listening shearers gape,
He tells the story o'er and o'er, and brags of his escape.
'Them barber chaps what keeps a tote, by George, I've had enough,
One tried to cut my bloomin' throat, but thank the Lord it's tough.'
And whether he's believed or no, there's one thing to remark,
That flowing beards are all the go way up in Ironbark.

A. B. PATERSON

REACT

Read each ballad as a whole class, then take some time to study them
individually. Decide which story or character appeals to you most.

1   Ask about any words or phrases in the ballads which you may not
     understand. Make a personal list of all the 'new-to-you' vocabulary in the
     poems.

2   Divide into three groups: those who preferred 'Mulga Bill's Bicycle';
     those who preferred 'The Man From Ironbark' and those who preferred
     'Holy Dan'. In these groups, prepare a case in support of your chosen
     ballad. Then, as a group, sit at the front of the class and 'sell' your ballad
     to the other two groups. Use a natural 'discussion-style' approach with
     each group member 'adding their piece' wherever appropriate. Decide
     which group presented the most convincing case.

3   Each of these ballads could be said to have a moral or message. Share
     your ideas about what this might be in each case.

RESPOND

1   Prepare an individual reading of 'Holy Dan' (see reading guidelines
     on page v). In your reading watch:
     (a) Emphasis. (In ballads, rhyme is used to create emphasis, so be sure to
          emphasise rhyming words.)
     (b) Alliteration. This also needs to be emphasised: 'All dry and
          <u>h</u>ot as <u>h</u>ell'.

(c) Pause – this will help to create interest and colour in your reading. Note the punctuation marks – they tell you the length of each pause.

(d) Repetition – this usually has a purpose and needs to be emphasised. It creates a rhythmic effect too.

or

2   In a group of three, enact 'The Man from Ironbark'. You will need the barber, his 'victim' and a narrator. Your classmate audience can act as the 'gilded youths that sat along the barber's wall'. Try as hard as you can (especially the barber and 'victim') to create real characters for your performance.

or

3   In pairs (Mulga Bill and narrator), prepare a dramatic reading of 'Mulga Bill's Bicycle'. The comments made in questions 1 and 2 are relevant to this reading also.

PAINTING
PICTURES

READ

Read these three personal poems as a whole class.

MYSELF

I am tall and fair
When I move I sometimes creak
It is natural I think.
I have lived a long eerie life.

KEN GODDARD

SELF PORTRAIT

How pleasant to know Mr Lear!
  Who has written such volumes of stuff!
Some think him ill-tempered and queer,
  But a few think him pleasant enough.

His mind is concrete and fastidious,
  His nose is remarkably big;
His visage is more or less hideous,
  His beard it resembles a wig.

He has ears, and two eyes, and ten fingers,
  Leastways, if you reckon two thumbs;
  Long ago he was one of the singers,
But now he is one of the dumbs.

He sits in a beautiful parlour,
  With hundreds of books on the wall;
He drinks a great deal of Marsala,
  But never gets tipsy at all.

He has many friends, laymen and clerical;
  Old Foss is the name of his cat;
His body is perfectly spherical,
  He weareth a runcible hat.

When he walks in a waterproof white,
  The children run after him so!
Calling out, 'He's come out in his night-
  Gown, that crazy old Englishman, oh!'

He weeps by the side of the ocean,
  He weeps on the top of the hill;
He purchases pancakes and lotion,
  And chocolate shrimps from the mill.

He reads but he cannot speak Spanish,
  He cannot abide ginger-beer:
Ere the days of his pilgrimage vanish,
  How pleasant to know Mr Lear!

EDWARD LEAR

NOT I

Some like drink
In a pint pot,
Some like to think;
        Some not.

Some like to laugh,
Some like to cry,
Some like chaff;
        Not I.

R. L. STEVENSON

REACT

In groups of four to six students, take about ten minutes to decide whether any of these poems are:
- strange
- beautiful
- creative
- original
- moody
- unusual
- unexpected
- well formed or structured as traditional poetry

or you may have different ideas!

Share your findings as a whole class.

RESPOND

Choose one of the following activities:

1   (a)   Model a personal poem on one of the poems above. (If you choose 'Self Portrait' your own version need not be as long – at least three verses though.)
            or
    (b)   From available class or library anthologies, make a collection of personal poems.
            or
    (c)   Create a 'poetic picture' of yourself. Take a large sheet of paper or cardboard and place a sketch or photograph of yourself in the centre. Now surround the picture with 'poetic phrases' about yourself.

You might include, for example, a pair of rhyming lines (called a 'couplet'); for example:

I am short and squat.
When I think, I think a lot.

You might concoct some alliterative (see page 146) phrases; such as 'taut, trim and terrific'; 'silently sombre, seriously studious'. You could create an unusual image or word picture; for example: 'scrawny, shadowy limbs'; 'as dumb as an ageing ass', 'calm as a marble'.

READ

Here we have a series of simple yet beautiful little poems. Each is an image, a picture captured in a few brief lines.

FIRST FROST, CRISP, DOGLESS HOUR

Still park near middle night
The wallaby down on all fours
on the sweet wet scented grass

moves only his mouth
The moon squats down to look
– there – between the two front paws –
is it moonlight he is eating
is it grassblades

J. S. HARRY

CITY SCENE

See-saw sky-scraper,
pocked with holes like
a nutmeg grater.

BEVERLEY HARRY

29

A FLOCK OF LITTLE BOATS

A flock of little boats
Tethered to the shore
Drifts in still water ...
Prows dip, nibbling.

SAMUEL MENASHE

SUNDAY MORNING

Sunday morning

      and the sun
      bawls
      with
      his big mouth

Yachts

      paper triangles
      of white and blue
      crowd the sloping bay
      appearing motionless
      as if stuck there
      by some infant thumb

      beneath a shouting sky

      upon a painted sea

WES MAGEE

REACT

Discuss each poem in pairs. Decide what is special about each – is it an
unusual or highly evocative word (a word that says or depicts a lot)?
An image or word picture – perhaps a metaphor or simile (see page 147)?
The use of personification, when an inanimate object or thing is described
as if it were a person? What about the way the poem is formed into particular
lines, its overall shape or form?

RESPOND

In pairs, try a short poem of your own which focuses on a single image. Note how each of the above poets has changed a simple sight – anchored boats, a nibbling wallaby, yachts on the sea, and a skyscraper – into a few memorable lines.

You should note too that the finished product may not have come easily. The poet probably had to work on the image, to create at least a couple of 'doodles and drafts' before he or she achieved the final effect.

It may take you a week to achieve anything worthwhile but, if you are prepared to work at it, you may surprise yourself.

So, work together on one brief poem or image. Look around you carefully. As you've seen above, the simplest sights can inspire beautiful poetry.

Mount a class display of your efforts.

READ

Each of the following descriptions are vivid impressions of natural events – a storm and the night.

COMING HOME

Driving home in the car
   Cosy and warm
   Through the storm.

Wipers pierce the beads
   Of curtained rain
   Again and again.

Fierce black traffic beasts
   Beam to the skies
   Their blinding eyes.

Bright traffic lights drip
   Red and green streaks
   Into road creeks.

Tyres splurt and splash
   Zig-zag and swerve
   Round the curve.

Huge shadowy limbs
  Of trees in the park
  Grasp at the dark.

Warm milk by the fire
  Safe from the blast
  Home at last.

JOAN M. SHILTON

NIGHT

Fewer cars to break
this quiet.
Lights appear and
vanish.
The pauses lengthen.

Birds folding feathers
keep their
songs snug till
morning.
An aeroplane drones.

A rustle of voices
hovers on
the edge of rooftops.
Cats slink
round waiting milkbottles.

The clock insists,
trying
to tell me something
I fear
but cannot name.

ERIC WILLIAMS

32

REACT

In groups of four to six students, try to come to agreement on the
following issue:
• What is the most noticeable poetic feature of each poem? (Its form or
  shape? Its imagery? Its creativity? Its mood? Its rhyme? Its rhythm?).

Together, choose the single most dominant feature for each poem: you must all agree.

You will need to consider these guidelines for effective discussion and agreement:

- Listen carefully to each other.
- Don't assume you are right; keep an open mind until you've heard everybody's opinion.
- Don't proffer an opinion without supporting it.
- Encourage comments from students who may not feel as confident in discussion as you do.

Elect a student in each group to report back to the whole class.

RESPOND

1 (a) Use one of the following images from the poems above as the beginning of a 'moody', descriptive prose paragraph of your own. Concentrate on maintaining the mood with appropriate images and evocative vocabulary.

> Wipers pierce the beads
>   Of curtained rain
>   Again and again
>
> A rustle of voices
> hovers on
> the edge of rooftops.

or

(b) Write five moody images of your own. Use both the three-line, rhyming form of 'Coming Home':

> Huge shadowy limbs
>   Of trees in the park
>   Grasp at the dark.

and the free-verse form (see page 146) of 'Night':

> Birds folding feathers
> keep their
> songs snug till
> morning.

Decide carefully, if you are writing free verse, where you will start and finish your lines. It makes an enormous difference to the sound and mood of the image, as you will see if you experiment.

(You may wish to use one form only and combine your five images as a complete poem.)

33

READ

Throughout history, poets have celebrated the seasons in their verse. Here is a simply patterned poem about autumn.

AUTUMN

Whirling leaves, golden and brown,
Twisting and turning,
Hurrying down.

Driving wind, gusty and strong,
Whistling and sighing,
Rushing along.

Scudding clouds, grey-leaden sky,
Laughing and playing,
Galloping by.

Roaming birds, gathered for flight,
Chirping and preening,
Seeking sunlight.

Curling smoke, mindful of fires,
Blowing and puffing,
Hiding the spires.

Drooping rose, scattered to earth,
Dying and fading,
Waiting new birth.

F. POLITZER

REACT

1   What elements of pattern are repeated in each verse?

2   Do you think the patterned form makes the poem more interesting or less so?

RESPOND

1   Write your own 'seasonal' poem, following this pattern or, if you're feeling really creative, a pattern that you devise for yourself.
    or

2   Find a seasonal poem about your own country and, by contrast, one
about another country. (Two poems about the same season would be
ideal but if this proves impossible, any two seasons will do.)

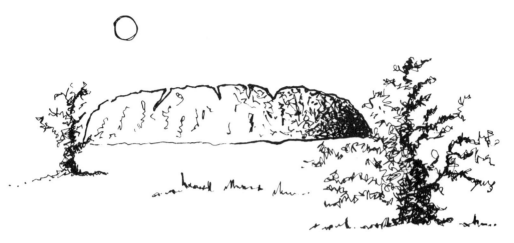

READ

This compact little poem has obvious poetic features – a definite form or
shape, a rhyme pattern, a meaningful movement or rhythm, and some
cleverly chosen words and phrases.

35

BRONZE AND SILVER

Look
Where the land lies,
Open like a book
Beneath these evening skies;
Still and clear
The stars of September appear
One by shimmering one,
The bronze day done.

Listen
How the birds sing
When the dew drops glisten,
The morning skies murmuring;
Soft and clear
The songs of September appear,
One by trembling one,
The silver day begun.

LEONARD CLARK

REACT

Form small groups of four to six students and decide:

1   Why the poem is called 'Bronze and Silver'.

2   How the pattern of the first verse is repeated in the pattern of the second verse.

3   Which words and phrases in the poem are particularly important to the poem's mood and feeling.

As a whole class, share your findings.

RESPOND

1   Write your own 'look and listen' poem.
   or
2   Write a similarly patterned poem using two of our other senses – perhaps 'taste and smell' or 'feel and hear'.
   or
3   Find two pictures or paintings that you consider to be illustrations of the poem. If possible, one should illustrate the first verse; the other, the second verse.

READ

Three poems this time, about three very different women. Read them together as a whole class.

WARNING

When I am an old woman I shall wear purple
With a red hat which doesn't go, and doesn't suit me.
And I shall spend my pension on brandy and summer gloves
And satin sandals, and say we've no money for butter.
I shall sit down on the pavement when I'm tired
And gobble up samples in shops and press alarm bells
And run my stick along the public railings
And make up for the sobriety of my youth.
I shall go out in my slippers in the rain
And pick the flowers in other people's gardens
And learn to spit.

You can wear terrible shirts and grow more fat
And eat three pounds of sausages at a go
Or only bread and pickle for a week
And hoard pens and pencils and beermats and things in boxes.

But now we must have clothes that keep us dry
And pay our rent and not swear in the street
And set a good example for the children.
We must have friends to dinner and read the papers.

But maybe I ought to practise a little now?
So people who know me are not too shocked and surprised
When suddenly I am old, and start to wear purple.

JENNY JOSEPH

SONNET

to my grandmother

She sat rock solid at the round table
a huge arm on the dresser plucking cups
like apples. Not stirring she was able
to command three generations, their ups
and downs soothed or frozen by Irish blue
eyes and serrated brogue. Rules were stone cast,
she was right and that was that, we all knew
first in was awarded the cherry, last
an icy word. Her kitchen was centre
of Christendom, food but an irksome chore
beyond concern. Talk, song, and gin lent her
power of the moon, we a tide to her shore.
All other rooms were exile, shells to hold
to an ear where her laughter sounded cold.

JOHN FAIRFAX

37

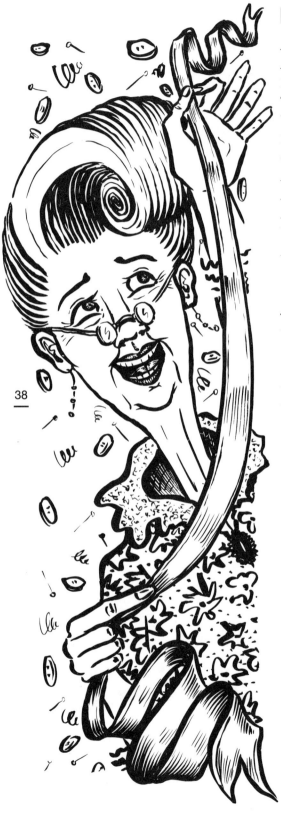

MISS WING

At the end of the street lives small Miss Wing,
A feathery, fluttery bird of a thing.
If you climb the street to the very top,
There you will see her fancy shop
With ribbons and buttons and frills and fluffs,
Pins and needles, purses and puffs,
Cosies and cushions and bits of chiffon,
And tiny hankies for ladies to sniff on,
And twists of silk and pieces of lace,
And odds and ends all over the place.
You push the door and the door-bell rings,
And the voice you hear is little Miss Wing's.
'Good-day, my dear, and how do you do?
Now tell me, what can I do for you?
Just half a second, please, dear Miss Gay –
As I was saying the other day –
Now what did I do with that so-and-so?
I'm sure I had it a moment ago –
As I was saying – why, yes, my dear –
A very nice day for the time of the year –
Have you heard how poor Mrs Such-and-such? –
Oh, I hope I haven't charged too much;
That would never do – Now, what about pink?
It's nice for children, I always think –
Some buttons to go with a lavender frock?
Why now, I believe I'm out of stock –
Well, what about these? Oh, I never knew –
I'm ever so sorry – now what about blue?
Such a very nice woman – a flower for a hat?'
And so she goes on, with 'Fancy that!'
And 'You never can tell,' and 'Oh dear, no,'
And 'There now! It only goes to show.'
And on she goes like a hank of tape,
A reel of ribbon, a roll of crêpe
Till you think her tongue will never stop.
And that's Miss Wing of the fancy shop.

JAMES REEVES

38

REACT

As a whole class (seated in a circle facing each other if possible), share your thoughts and opinions on these points:

1   Which poem (or character) appeals to you the most?. Can you explain why?

2   Each poem has a different mood or feeling. Can you find a word (or words) to describe the mood in each case?

3   'Warning' is written in free verse (see page 146), and the word 'and' has been used frequently. Why do you think the poet has written the poem in this way?

4   Look at 'Sonnet', written for the poet's grandmother. A sonnet is a traditional form of poetry – sonnets have 14 lines and a particular rhyming pattern. Can you see where the rhyming pattern changes? Why do you think the poet has chosen a traditional form for this poem?

5   In the first seven lines of 'Miss Wing', the poet uses a lot of alliteration. Does this help him create the mood for his poem?

RESPOND

Choose one of these follow-up activities:

1   Write a paragraph or two of prose to describe your favourite character from the three poems. Draw your information from the poem and try to capture its particular mood or feeling in your writing too. Remember, prose can be just as 'moody' as poetry.
    or

2   Choose one of the poems as your model and write about an interesting male character. It may be someone you know or a product of your imagination.
    or

3   Prepare an individual reading of 'Warning' or 'Sonnet'. (See reading guidelines on page v.)
    • Look out for the pauses (commas and full stops).
    • Look out for the run-on lines; don't actually pause here for any length of time but let your voice 'hang a little in the air' while you 'run-on' to the next line. Usually, if you emphasise the last word in each line or the first word of the following line – choose whichever you feel is right – you will create the right effect.
    • Emphasise the verbs, which help the poet highlight the action in the poem. 'Sonnet' has some very telling verbs: 'sat rock solid', 'plucking cups/like apples', and 'Warning' is crammed full of verbs.

or

4 Prepare a reading of 'Miss Wing' in pairs. One student reads Miss Wing's dialogue whilst the other becomes the narrator and reads the remaining parts. (See reading guidelines on page v.) For this reading consider:
   • rhyme, rhythm, run-on lines and alliteration (see notes for other poems in question 3)
   • assuming a voice that would suit Miss Wing's character
   • assuming a voice that would suit the narrator's character.

MAKING YOU AWARE

READ

These poems explore at least five contemporary (current) issues that affect the way we live.

ESTATE

Mother!
They're building a towncentre in the bedroom
A carpark in the lounge, it's a sin.

There's a block of flats going up in the toilet
What a shocking estate we are in.

ROGER McGOUGH

MAD AD

A Madison Avenue whizzkid
thought it a disgrace
That no-one had exploited
the possibilities in space
Discussed it with a client
who agreed and very soon
A thousand miles of neontubing
were transported to the moon.

Now no-one can ignore it
the product's selling fine
The night they turned the moon
into a Coca-Cola sign.

ROGER McGOUGH

FATE'S TOOLS

The whole wide world is terrible
The litter is unbearable
The bottles aren't returnable
The empty cans aren't burnable
The sonic boom's incredible
The fish no longer edible
The off-shore rigs are leakable
The billboards are unspeakable
The slumlords are incurable
The smog is unendurable
The phosphates aren't dissolvable
The problems are unsolvable
The mess is unforgivable
Let's face it – life's unlivable.

GEOFFREY LUNGREN

IT'S POISONING DOWN

Granny keeps telling stories
Of how she used to go
Walking in the pouring rain
And playing in the snow.
She talks of things called flowers.
She says they had nice smells.
(Sometimes she sounds convincing,
The crazy fibs she tells!)
She says that lakes and rivers
Were once all clean and pure,
But I don't believe a word,
I've heard it all before.
Poor Gran can be quite dotty –
You want to see Mum frown
When she tries to get outside
Even though it's poisoning down.

We've had to fit 'Granny Locks'
To keep poor Granny in.
She really doesn't understand
How rain eats away the skin.

BRIAN PATTEN

43

REACT

- Read the poems as a whole class and list the issues they deal with.
- Six students volunteer to form a panel and *each* chooses *one* of these roles to play:

   The director of a chemical plant.
   A timber cutter.
   A developer.
   An advertising executive.
   The Minister for the Environment.

The rest of the class is divided into six small groups. Each group prepares a series of questions, comments or accusations to direct to one of the panel members in role. When preparing your questions, refer back to the poems for information and inspiration.

- To prepare themselves, the six panel members should consider their positions and likely questions or criticisms in advance. They should be prepared, as politicians are, to rebut or 'explain away' this criticism.

- Stage your panel – audience discussion for as long as it has some 'fire'.

RESPOND

1 'It's Poisoning Down' is written from an imaginary nightmare future. Write a poem about a conservation issue that worries or disturbs you, as if you were writing 100 years from now. It doesn't have to be depressing: you might want to make the future better, not worse, in your poem.

or

2 Make a collage to illustrate the issue of *visual pollution*, an issue raised by both 'Mad Ad' and 'Fate's Tools'. Include comments, verse, photographs, news clippings – whatever you can gather and arrange to represent the issue creatively.

or

3 Make a poster to campaign about one of the issues raised in the poems. Remember that a poster should be uncluttered and 'arresting'.
Any message (or wording) should be short and sharp and, if possible, moving and memorable.

44

READ

Here we have three stark, simple poems about a horrific event – war.

OTHER PEOPLE

In the First World War they ...
Who were *they*? Who cares any more?...
Killed four of my uncles,
So I discovered one day.

There were only four on that side of the family
And all swept away in a few bad years
In a war the historians tell us now
Was fought over nothing at all.

Four uncles, as one might say
A dozen apples or seven tons of dirt,
Swept away by the luck of history,
Closed off. Full stop.

Four is a lot for uncles,
A lot for lives, I should say.
Their chalk was wiped clean off the slate,
The War meant nothing at all.

War needs a lot of uncles,
And husbands, and brothers, and so on:
Someone must *want* to kill them,
Somebody needs them dead.

Who is it, I wonder. Me?
Or is it you there, reading away,
Or a chap with a small-arms factory?
Or is it only *they*?

CHRIS WALLACE-CRABBE

45

LOST IN FRANCE
JO'S REQUIEM

He had the ploughman's strength
in the grasp of his hand;
He could see a crow
three miles away,
and the trout beneath the stone.
He could hear the green oats growing,
and the south-west wind making rain.
He could hear the wheel upon the hill
When it left the level road.
He could make a gate, and dig a pit,
and plough as straight as stone can fall.
And he is dead.

ERNEST RHYS

BUT YOU DIDN'T

Remember the time you lent me your car and I dented it?
I thought you'd kill me ...
But you didn't.

Remember the time I forgot to tell you the dance was
formal, and you came in jeans?
I thought you'd hate me ...
But you didn't.

Remember the times I'd flirt with
other boys just to make you jealous, and
you were?
I thought you'd drop me ...
But you didn't.

There were plenty of things you did to put up with me,
to keep me happy, to love me, and there are
so many things I wanted to tell
you when you returned from
Vietnam ...
But you didn't.

MERRILL GLASS

REACT

In groups of four to six students, consider these questions:

1   Each poem has one particularly impactful, most important line.
    What is it in each case?

2   Complete each of the sentences below to express each poem's theme
    or topic.
    (a) 'Lost in France'
         The poet is indirectly saying that everyone is ...
    (b) 'Other People'
         The poet is asking us to consider ...
    (c) 'But You Didn't'
         This poem reminds us that ...

3   Find three words that could be used to describe all of these poems.
    In other words, you will be 'summarising' their similarities. Pool your
    results as a whole class.

RESPOND

1   Have you ever experienced the death of someone dear to you? If you have, write a 'Requiem' (a piece written to commemorate the dead) for him or her. As Ernest Rhys has done, try to emphasise the person's individuality and 'specialness'. You might like to follow his form, and use the same hard-hitting final line, or find an appropriate form of your own.
or

2   Choose appropriate lines from one or more of the poems to use as the centrepiece of a peace poster that you design yourself.
or

3   Interview someone you know who has been involved with war in some way or another. Draw up a list of questions to ask about:
details of their involvement;
their feelings or 'scars';
their attitudes to war both then and now.
Play the recorded interview to the class or write it up and display it in the classroom.

READ

These four simple poems form part of an increasing body of writing that attacks man's treatment of other living creatures.

47

LION

The lion is called the king
Of beasts. Nowadays there are
Almost as many lions
In cages as out of them.
If offered a crown, refuse.

KENNETH REXROTH

DEER

Deer are gentle and graceful
And they have beautiful eyes.
They hurt no one but themselves,
The males, and only for love.
Men have invented several
Thousand ways of killing them.

KENNETH REXROTH

THE CAGED BIRD IN SPRINGTIME

What can it be,
This curious anxiety?
It is as if I wanted
To fly away from here.

But how absurd!
I have never flown in my life,
And I do not know
What flying means, though I have heard,
Of course, something about it.

Why do I peck the wires of this little cage?
It is the only nest I have ever known.
But I want to build my own,
High in the secret branches of the air.

I cannot quite remember how
It is done, but I know
That what I want to do
Cannot be done here.

I have all I need –
Seed and water, air and light.
Why, then, do I weep with anguish,
And beat my head and my wings
Against those sharp wires, while the children
Smile at each other, saying: 'Hark how he sings'?

JAMES KIRKUP

THE WHIPTAIL WALLABY

PRETTY FACE

Where eucalyptus trees are tall, and tower on every side
Below the rocky eastern wall that forms the Great Divide

And messmate grows with mountain ash above the ferns and grasses,
Through shadowed gullies like a flash the little whiptail passes.

His head is small and fine as lace, all striped in white and yellow.
The bushmen call him Pretty Face, he's such a handsome fellow.

48

His coat is grey as winter skies, with white on hips and shoulders,
And swift as any bird he flies between the rocks and boulders.

He's very active, small and shy, and naturalists salute him,
And I have often wondered why the 'sportsmen' what to shoot him.

He quietly roams the bushland wide, and harms no other creature,
But shooters think to lift his hide is quite a sporting feature.

So oft his body you will find, hung over fence and sliprail,
A 'sport' must have a weak, sick mind to want to kill the whiptail.

KEITH GARVEY

REACT

Use the poems at the starting point for a whole class discussion of humans'
treatment of other living creatures. Refer to the poems to support your
discussion where relevant. Below are some guidelines for effective discussion.

DISCUSSION GUIDELINES

1 Choose six students who will act as observers of the group discussion.
   Assign each of these six an equal number of particular students to
   observe. They are to report back on those students' discussion skills:
   • How much did each student contribute?
   • Did they listen and respond to what others actually said or were they
     only concerned with their own comments and opinions?
   • Did they try to dominate the discussion or were they willing listeners
     as well as good contributors?
   • Did anyone make any comments that were particularly helpful to the
     discussion?

2 Those who are participants in the discussion are to sit in one large circle
   so that they are in eye contact. Observers sit outside this circle.

3 Continue the discussion for fifteen to twenty minutes, allowing time for
   the observers to comment.

RESPOND

1 Write about another animal in the style of 'The Caged Bird In
   Springtime'. What are the animal's thoughts, feelings and natural
   desires?
   or

49

2   Write in response to one of these topics:
  • If I could talk to the animals ...
  • Man and his animal ways
  • Animal liberation – pros and cons.
  or
3   Find out what you can about the animal liberation movement. Write a research report, using this outline as a guide:
  • What is animal liberation?
  • Describe its aims, membership, various groups/branches and some causes or activities;
  • Write a summary and conclusion.

READ

Here we have three different poems each concerned with a very broad issue – that of bombing.

THE RESPONSIBILITY

I am the man who gives the word,
If it should come, to use the Bomb,
I am the man who spreads the word
From him to them if it should come.

I am the man who gets the word
From him who spreads the word from him.

I am the man who drops the Bomb
If ordered to by one who's heard
From him who merely spreads the word
The first one gives if it should come.

I am the man who loads the Bomb
That he must drop should orders come
From him who gets the word passed on
By one who waits to hear from him.

I am the man who makes the Bomb
That he must load for him to drop
If told by one who gets the word
From one who passes it from him.

I am the man who fills the till,
Who pays the tax, who foots the bill
That guarantees the Bomb he makes
For him to load for him to drop
If orders come from one who gets
The word passed on to him by one
Who waits to hear it from the man
Who gives the word to use the Bomb.

I am the man behind it all;
I am the one responsible.

PETER APPLETON

KILL THE CHILDREN

On Hallowe'en in Ship Street,
quite close to Benny's bar,
the children lit a bonfire
and the adults parked a car.
Sick minds sing sentimental songs
and speak in dreary prose
and make ingenious home-made bombs –
and this was one of those.

Some say it was the UVF
and some the IRA
blew up that pub on principle
and killed the kids at play.

They didn't mean the children,
it only was the blast;
we call it KILL THE CHILDREN DAY
in bitter old Belfast.

JAMES SIMMONS

FIFTEEN MILLION PLASTIC BAGS

I was walking in a government warehouse
Where the daylight never goes.
I saw fifteen million plastic bags
Hanging in a thousand rows.

51

Five million bags were six feet long
Five million bags were five foot five
Five million were stamped with Mickey Mouse
And they came in a smaller size.

Were they for guns or uniforms
Or a kinky kind of party game?
Then I saw each bag had a number
And every bag bore a name.

And five million bags were six feet long
Five million were five foot five
Five million were stamped with Mickey Mouse
And they came in a smaller size

So I've taken my bag from the hanger
And I've pulled it over my head
And I'll wait for the priest to zip it
So the radiation won't spread

Now five million bags are six feet long
Five million are five foot five
Five million are stamped with Mickey Mouse
And they come in a smaller size.

ADRIAN MITCHELL

REACT

'FIFTEEN MILLION PLASTIC BAGS'

1   The poet has used repetition to great effect in this poem. Why do you think it is so effective?

2   The poem is in simple, stark language. Do you think this works? In what way does it help the poet to get his message across?

3   Which line in the poem do you think is the most sinister? Why?

'THE RESPONSIBILITY'

1   Name at least four people who are, according to the poet, responsible for the bomb. Is anyone particularly responsible? Who is the 'man behind it all'?

2   Do you agree with the poet's point of view?

3　This poem is based on a children's rhyme – do you know it? You might like to copy both the children's rhyme and 'The Responsibility' into your workbook.

'KILL THE CHILDREN'

1　Explain what 'ingenious' and 'on principle' mean in the poem.

2　Discuss the irony (see page 146) of committing such acts of violence 'on principle'.

3　Is this poem effective? In other words, does it have an effect on you? If so, can you explain what and why?

4　What do you think of the poem's title? What does it lead you to expect about the poem?

5　What effect does the last line have? Why?

RESPOND

1　Prepare a radio news item and a newspaper report on the events described in 'Kill the Children'. You may add details to develop your newspaper report if you like. A radio news item, on the other hand, is brief and factual – it answers the questions: who? what? when? where? why?
　or

2　It's not only bombing that causes radiation – nuclear accidents can, too. Do some research into those at Chernobyl, Russia, or Five Mile Island, America. Then research the benefits of nuclear power in peacetime. Write up your results in a research paper, 'Nuclear Power – A Personal View'.
　or

3　Form groups of six students and prepare and present a formal debate on the topic: that we are all responsible for the bomb. You will need to decide which three students will form the affirmative side (yes, we are all responsible) and which three will debate the negative side (no, we are not all responsible).

53

READ

Contemporary poets are often critical of the way we live and of the sorts of lives we lead. In each of the following poems, people are seen as automated, unthinking robots rather than rational human beings.

DAILY LONDON RECIPE

Take any number of them
you can think of,
pour into empty red bus
       until full,
and then push in
       ten more.
Allow enough time
to get hot under the collar
before transferring into
multistorey building.
Leave for eight hours,
and pour back into same bus
      already half full.
      Scrape remainder off.
When settled down
tip into terraced houses each
carefully lined with copy
of *The Standard* and *Tit Bits*.
Place mixture before open
television screen at 7 p.m.
and then allow to cool
in bed at 10.30 p.m.
May be served with
working overalls
or pinstripe suit.

STEVE TURNER

54

LETTER FROM LILLIPUT

The people travel everywhere enclosed by walls.
Their metal houses built on wheels, complete
With windows, doors, serve them as shells
Serve hermit-crabs. These are their floating
Islands, which they navigate themselves
Along the grey canals, sleek and upholstered,
Chromium-plated realms where they alone
Can reign, a small extension of their privacy,
A home away from home.
Some are on business, others out
For sights, and some would seek escape,
As if by travelling fast enough they leave
Time far behind them, and all their
Worries fly away like gravel from beneath
Their tyres: an idle dream.
I have watched them, from the footpath,
Flashing by imprisoned behind glass.
Sometimes they remind me of grubs
Inside cocoons, waiting impatiently
The freedom of bright wings,
But much more frequently of fish within
A sealed tank, staring out
With glazed, incomprehending eyes
At creatures moving in a different element.

JOHN PAISLEY

REACT

'DAILY LONDON RECIPE'

1   In this poem, the poet is clearly regarding people as things – as ingredients
    in a recipe – rather than as human beings. List all the examples you can find
    of language which you would expect to find in a recipe. What does such
    language indicate about the poet's attitude?

2   How does the poet's treatment of human beings as ingredients in a recipe
    help to convey his message or theme (see page 147)? What is this theme? Do
    you agree with it?

'LETTER FROM LILLIPUT'

1   This poem is written as though it were a letter from a visitor to the
    imaginary kingdom of Lilliput, like a tourist's description of a foreign
    city. Is this a suitable form (see page 146) for the poet's topic, do you think?

2   What do you think the poet feels about our lifestyle? Do you agree
     with him?

3   Read the last seven lines carefully. Why do you think the poet has
     changed his metaphor (see page 147) from 'grubs inside cocoons' to 'fish
     within a sealed tank'?

RESPOND

1   Write your own recipe poems using a form similar to that of 'Daily
     London Recipe'. Here is one suggestion:

Study Recipe (for disaster!)
Take any number of facts
you can find,
Cram into peabrain
            until exhausted
and then squeeze in
              ten more.
etc.

          Or you may choose, as the poet did, to make a 'comment' about the
     way we live:

Daily Recipe
Take a day of the week
And sift it with sleepiness.
Pour in a bad temper
Then beat until smooth.
Add ...
etc.

          Don't follow the original form in every detail if you don't want to.
     Invent your own form!
     or

2   Write a 'poetic letter' from outer space. Try to see some aspect of life on
     earth through the eyes of an extraterrestrial stranger, as John Paisley
     has done. You might start by brainstorming as a whole class those
     aspects of our lives (or ourselves) that could seem odd, pointless or
     puzzling to an 'outsider'.
     or

3   Write about one A4 page or so of prose inspired by one of these titles:
     • Day in and day out ...
     • A bird's-eye view.
     • Crazy but true.
     • Mindless machines.

EXPRESSING THOUGHTS AND FEELINGS

READ

The following poems reflect on different subjects in very different ways.

THESE HAVE I LOVED

These have I loved:
　　　　White plates and cups, cleaning-gleaming,
Ringed with blue lines; and feathery, faery dust;
Wet roofs beneath the lamp-light; the strong crust
Of friendly bread; and many-tasting food;

Rainbows; and the blue bitter smoke of wood;
And radiant raindrops couching in cool flowers;
And flowers themselves, that sway through sunny hours,
Dreaming of moths that drink them under the moon ...
Sweet water's dimpling laugh from tap or spring;
Holes in the ground; and voices that do sing:
Voices in laughter, too; and body's pain.

RUPERT BROOKE

CLOTHES

My mother keeps on telling me
When she was in her teens
She wore quite different clothes from mine
And hadn't heard of jeans,

T-shirts, no hats, and dresses that
Reach far above our knees.
I laughed at first and then I thought
One day my kids will tease

And scoff at what *I'm* wearing now.
What will *their* fashions be?
I'd give an awful lot to know,
To look ahead and see.

Girls dressed like girls perhaps once more
And boys no longer half
Resembling us. Oh, what's in store
To make *our* children laugh?

ELIZABETH JENNINGS

REACT

1 Although 'Clothes' is a lighthearted, simple poem, it has a theme or message. Express this idea as succinctly (briefly and to the point) as you can, in one sentence.

2 'These Have I Loved' is really only a list, yet it is artfully and poetically arranged. Discuss what you consider to be the poem's artful or poetic features.

RESPOND

1 Have a whole class discussion about things (apart from fashion) that have changed dramatically in the last ten years. Then consider how these and other things may change even more dramatically in the future. Use this discussion as the basis of a personal essay with one of the following titles:
   • One day *my* kids will tease.
   • To look ahead and see ...
   • What's in store?
   • Yesterday, today and tomorrow.
   or

2 (a) Fill a page with jottings of all the things you love. Think of people, places, sights, sounds, smells, tastes and feelings.
   (b) Now go back and choose the jottings that you consider to be the most unusual.
   (c) Look back to the poem, 'These Have I Loved', and notice the detail again. The poet didn't simply love 'wet roofs', but 'wet roofs beneath the lamplight' and 'white plates and cups, cleaning-gleaming'. Can you make your selected jottings more descriptive, detailed or precise?
   (d) When you have done this, arrange your results in a suitable piece of prose or poetry.

59

READ

Each of these three poems reflects on personal experience, expressing thoughts, feelings and impressions in a natural, descriptive way.

Freewheeling on a bike –
and butterflies of sunlight
all over me.

ROBERT GRAY

HAPPINESS

60

lying in bed ofa weekdaymorning
Autumn
and the trees
none the worse for it.
Youve just got up
to make tea toast and a bottle
leaving pastures warm
for me to stretch into

in his cot
the littlefella
outsings the birds

Plenty of honey in the cupboard.
Nice.

ROGER McGOUGH

WHISPER WHISPER

whisper whisper
whisper whisper
goes my sister
down the phone

whisper whisper
go the beech leaves
breathing in the
wind alone

whisper whisper
whisper whisper
slips the river
on the stone

whisper whisper
go my parents
when they whisper
on their own

I don't mind the
whisper whisper
whisper whisper
it's a tune

sometimes though
I wish the whisper
whisperings would
shut up soon

KIT WRIGHT

REACT

1   'Freewheeling...' is nothing more than one clever metaphor (see page 147). Do you think it is an appropriate one?

2   What do you like most of all about 'Happiness'? Why? What is the effect of the understatement in the lines 'Autumn/and the trees/none the worse for it'?

3   Why do you think the poet has repeated the words 'whisper whisper' in his poem of the same title? Why is the last line so effective?

RESPOND

1   Think of your favourite pastime – preferably an active one. Make this the first line of your poem, then create a single metaphor which seems to you to sum up what you like about that pastime. Use it in a three-line poem similar to 'Freewheeling'. Here is another one to inspire you:

> Walking in the early dawn –
> Cobwebs of dewdrops
> Snare my shoeless feet

or

2   Think of a cosy, happy experience like the simple one described in 'Happiness'. Use a similar form – the 'combined' words; the short, summary last line; the different verses – and capture your experience in a similar, short poem.

or

3   In 'Whisper Whisper' the poet talks about very different kinds of whispering. In prose or poetry, write about just one 'whispering' experience you've had.

READ

Here we have a series of simple reflections about the natural world.

THE KESTREL

How often I have stood
To see her climb the sky,
Teasing the slow sun,
Printing a pattern of wings
On the earth below.

I found her dead beside the road,
Wings closed to her side,
Only my sigh stirred
The feathers of her breast.
I felt as though the winds themselves
Lay dead within my hand.

ANNE BELL

THE BEE

The bee is a merchant.
He trades among
flower planets.

PETER KELSO

THE WIND

The wind is a dog
flattening all this tall grass
before lying down.

KEVIN HART

RIVER WINDING

Rain falling, what things do you grow?
Snow melting, where do you go?
Wind blowing, what trees do you know?
River winding, where do you flow?

CHARLOTTE ZOLOTOW

All day I hear the noise of waters
    Making moan,
Sad as the seabird is when going
    Forth alone
He hears the winds cry to the waters'
    Monotone.

The grey winds, the cold winds are blowing
    Where I go.
I hear the noise of many waters
    Far below.
All day, all night, I hear them flowing
    To and fro.

JAMES JOYCE

REACT

1   In pairs, decide which poem is the most
    * unusual
    * powerful
    * rhythmic
    * reflective.

2   In each of the following are images of one kind or another:
    * 'The wind is a dog' (metaphor)
    * 'The bee is a merchant' (metaphor)

- 'flower planets' (metaphor)
- 'All day I hear the noise of waters making moan' (aural image or image that describes sound). (See page 146.)
- 'Printing a pattern of wings/On the earth below.' (visual image or an image that describes sights). (See page 147.)

Decide, again in pairs, which of these images you consider to be the most effective. Compare your choices as a whole class.

RESPOND

1 Collect an anthology of four short poems about the natural world, similar to those above. Write up an assessment of your collection, using the following guidelines.

(a) Decide which poem is the most unusual, the most powerful, the most rhythmic and the most reflective. Support your decision in each case.

(b) From your collection of poems select at least four images that you think are effective. Discuss how each image achieves its effect and say which is your favourite and why.

or

- Use 'The Kestrel' as a model for your own poem about an endangered species; or
- Use 'The Wind' or 'The Bee' as the model for your own 'metaphor poem' about an aspect of the natural world; or
- Use 'All Day I Hear' as the model for a poem based on aural or sound imagery of the natural world; or
- Ask a series of questions about the natural word to form a rhythmic, rhyming verse similar to 'River Winding'.

READ

These poems are reflections – one on a personal future when love and youth have faded and the other on the future of our environment.

WHEN YOU ARE OLD

When you are old and gray and full of sleep,
And nodding by the fire, take down this book,
And slowly read, and dream of the soft look
Your eyes had once, and of their shadows deep;

How many loved your moments of glad grace,
And loved your beauty with love false or true;
But one man loved the pilgrim soul in you,
And loved the sorrows of your changing face.

And bending down beside the glowing bars
Murmur, a little sadly, how love fled
And paced upon the mountains overhead
And hid his face amid a crown of stars.

W. B. YEATS

65

REFLECTIONS

The rolling empty sandhills,
The silent desert night,
A quiet dry Sahara
Reflecting moon's clear light.

Above the barren landscape,
Another empty plain,
White jewels set in deep purple
Reflecting the world's pain.

Untouched are both these places,
For now in any case,
How long before they're ruined
And lost without a trace?

How long before the desert
Is concrete instead of sand?
How long till stars surrender
To the space junk that we land?

No desert, nor the sky above,
Will ever get a say,
But for now they hold their secrets
In their quiet, empty way.

LARRAINE KIKKERT (student)

REACT

Write individual answers to these questions, then share these as a whole class.

'WHEN YOU ARE OLD'

1   This is a very 'moody' poem. Find a word or phrase that best sums up its mood and tone (see page 147).

2   List any words or phrases from the poem which you think help the poet create this mood or tone.

3   How does the rhyme pattern affect the mood?

4   Each line has ten syllables. What effect does this have on the poem's rhythm?

RESPOND

1   Find two more poems that reflect on the future. Collate the four poems
    (including these two) and draw or find a suitable picture or photograph
    to illustrate the theme of each poem. (Try to choose illustrations which
    are symbolic. For example, broken power lines could symbolise loss of
    speech or lack of communication; a dead tree could represent
    environmental decay.)
    or

2   'Reflections' was written by a student of about your own age, and
    reflects on the future of the environment. It may inspire you to reflect on
    the future in a similar way. Note that it has regular rhyme, rhythm and
    stanza pattern, as does 'When You Are Old'. You may decide on such
    a regular pattern for your own poem.

READ

Inanimate, everyday objects can sometimes be the inspiration for a reflective
piece of poetry. This one was written by a student of about your own age:

PIER

Your silhouette is black
Against the water –
You step into it
With one foot firmly on shore.
Your body is caterpillar-like
And your legs
As a caterpillar
Claw into the ocean
At regular,
Poised
Intervals.

To walk you
Is to hear
A memory
From someone who once stopped here.
Your moanings leave me uneasy.
Your rails splinter my hands.
Your boards are unsure.
The ocean breaks into you.
The cold wind showers me.

Why are you so, content to sit?
You are old, desolate, forgotten
And still you remain
A structure
To be restored
Again and again
'Til we forget.

SUZANNE ROGERS (student)

REACT

This poem grows out of the personification (see page 147) of the pier.
What evidence of this personification can you find?

RESPOND

1   Write a reflective poem in response to one of these photographs.
    Try to evoke a certain mood and explore the thoughts and feelings that
    the photograph stirs in you.

or

2   Write a reflective poem based on the personification of a particular place
    or object.
    or
3   Collect some similarly reflective poems.

CREATING

READ

All poems have some shape or form, but there are some which are written to fit a set form or pattern, made up of a specific number of lines and syllables, or a set order of different kinds of words. Here are some examples.

CINQUAINS

Cinquains must have five lines (*cinq* means five in French). There are two kinds of cinquains – one must have two syllables in the first line, four in the second, six in the third, eight in the fourth and two in the last line. For example:

Night comes
With cold, damp claws.
It lurks and depresses
The tramp with nowhere to shelter.
He coughs.

In the other kind of cinquain, the first line must consist of one word, which is also the subject of the poem; the second line must consist of two adjectives; the third of three adjectives; the fourth of a connected phrase; and the last of the one-word subject again. For example:

Poverty.
Cruel, chilling,
Solid, tireless, deathly.
Don't turn a blind eye,
Poverty.

SENSE FORMS

These are also five-line poems, but they concentrate on one or two senses and use alliteration (see page 146). Work out what the pattern is by looking closely at these examples.

The clock on the walls sounds
measured,
monotonous.
It ticks,
tocks.

The lemonade in the heat tastes
frosty,
fresh.
It soothes,
satisfies.

The beggar at the station looks
wretched,
ragged.
He pleads,
petitions.

The surf in summer feels
cool,
crisp;
it surges,
soothes.

HAIKU

A haiku must consist of three lines. Usually, the first line has five syllables, the second seven and the last five again. Here are some examples: see if you can spot the odd one out.

Tea-leaf in my cup:
did you read your own future,
growing in China?

Rain surprises us
like commas, punctuating
summer's flummery.

Elderberries hang
like a bunch of purple keys
unlocking wine.

SUE STEWART

REACT

As a whole class, try out some of these forms together, using blackboard and scribe to record your combined creative efforts.

RESPOND

1   Write one or more poems in *each* of the forms illustrated above.
    or

2   Be adventurous and invent a short form of your own. You will need
    to decide the number of lines and the 'content' of each line (for example,
    number of words, syllables or kinds of words – adjectives, phrases etc.)
    This is really quite simple to do and often leads to some very
    precise writing.
        When you have devised your form, create some poems to illustrate it.
    Share these with the rest of the class. (Did you give your form an
    appropriate name?)
    or

3   Find a poem, like the one below, that has an unusual, distinctive form.
    Write your poem in a similar form, but be careful to write on a topic that
    will suit the form.

THE WORLD IS A BEAUTIFUL PLACE

The world is a beautiful place
                              to be born into
    if you don't mind happiness
                          not always being
                                          so very much fun
        if you don't mind a touch of hell
                                      now and then
            just when everything is fine
                                          because even in heaven
                they don't sing
                                      all the time
            The world is a beautiful place
                                  to be born into
        if you don't mind some people dying
                                              all the time
                or maybe only starving
                                          some of the time
                which isn't half so bad
                                          If it isn't you.

LAWRENCE FERLINGHETTI

READ

The following poems are simple, creative expressions of writing for the fun
and pleasure of it.

NIGHT SCENE

out there where
the laurel hedge stood
there is a black wall
hiding in its
whispering buttresses
a blind panther
and a mad monk crouching
and a terror that
will take shape
the moment
you turn around
the fingered form
you see edging around

the corner of the tool shed
is dracula
frankenstein
the witch of endor
and a couple of werewolves
are talking in whispers
at the front gate
and every unexplored corner
of the dark
conceals a gibbering thing
not yet born
but lying in readiness
for the scream
of a horrible nightbird
that lives normally
in a sepulchre
when it screams
a thousand demons
will spring into awful life
wet winged
immense and pitiless
and batter the black air
with silent ferocity
the thing you see
over there to the right
in the pergola
is the ghost
of jack the ripper
this is what I say to
Morris Carmody
Morris is a little
thin nervous boy
he has been playing with me
tonight
as mother and father
are at the pictures
and he has to go home
by himself

REDMOND PHILLIPS

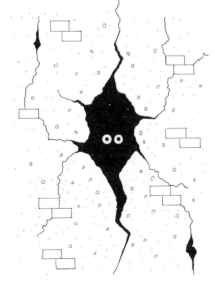

THE BALL

Can you catch?
Then watch while I throw it,
Up, ever so high.
White is the ball, so white
On the blue sky.

Run now,
Run under it, quick!
It's beginning to drop –
Drawn by the pull of the ground
To your two hand's cup.

Now you throw it yourself,
Higher yet.
Will it ever come down?
Will it float like a bubble all day
Over paddock and town?

But it hangs
Like a catch in the breath
While the moment expands,
Then faster and faster it speeds
To the cup of my hands.

LYDIA PENDER

MIDNIGHT

Midnight. Midnight. Midnight. Midnight.
Hark at the hands of the clock.

A knock of the sands on the glass of the grave,
A knock on the sands of the shore,
A knock on the horse's head of the wave,
A beggar's knock on the door.
A knock of a moth on the pane of light,
In the beat of the blood a knock.
Midnight. Midnight. Midnight. Midnight.
Hark at the hands of the clock.

The sands in the glass, the shrinking sands,
And the picklock, picklock, picklock hands.
Midnight. Midnight. Midnight. Midnight.
Hark at the hands of the clock.

VERNON WATKINS

REACT

1 'Night Scene' is a crazy poem with a most unexpected ending. What do you think of it?

2 'The Ball' is an immediate, creative description of the simple action of tossing a ball in the air. Are there any images which stand out? If so, why do you think they are effective?

3 See if you can work out the ways in which the poet creates the eerie mood of 'Midnight'.

4 Of the three poems, do you think that one is more successful than the others? Give reasons to justify your answer.

RESPOND

1 Make a collection of poems that seem to have been written for the sheer pleasure of responding to the world around. They will be short, uncomplicated, fresh and (seemingly) spontaneous.
   or

2 Write a poem about something as simple as the toss of a ball. Remember, as we saw in 'The Ball', it only takes one or two unusual lines or images to make a poem memorable.
   or

3   Write a poem like 'Night Scene' which is crazy and has an unexpected or matter-of-fact ending. Free verse (see page 146) is a suitable form for this kind of poem.

4   'Midnight' and 'Night Scene' might inspire a piece of prose writing for your journal.

READ

The following poems play with words in original and creative ways.

IF WORDS WERE BIRDS

If words
were birds
sentences
would fly
in formation
across page-white
skies.
Dictionaries would
have bars,
          speeches
would darken
the sun.
It words
were birds
fly formation

sentences

skies across

page white dictionaries.

Bars

would have speeches.

Blacken the

would

STEVE TURNER   sun.

EATING IS

Eating is
    hot chocolate that scorches the
tip of
    your
        tongue, but warms
                        your numb
                                    nose
        with a milky mocca m^{u}st^{a}ch$_e$
            impudent
        peas playing
                    go
            hide and   seek
        or
            a
                froli^{c}ki$_n$g tag with a
                        frustrated
                fork.
            hippopotamus HERO
            sandwiches
open
your mouth   W I D E
    but
        beware that the
insides
        do
            not
                fall
                    out.

    frothy fruit fillings
                in
    dignified fruit pies
    peeping
                out curious^{l}y from
                        beneath
                    the
            crust
oooooooooozzzing
                    out
            all
                over my fingers
        just
            so they can
                    go on a
        trip to the
            bathroom.

JESSICA TEICH

BRADFORD

The occasional curry

keeps

the

ɥɔɐɯoʇs

on

its

toes

ROGER McGOUGH

REACT

In small groups of four to six students, try to reach agreement on the following:

1   Which poem sounds the most poetic?

2   Which poem makes the most creative use of words?

3   Which poem makes the most creative use of space?

4   Which poem is the most contrived (least natural)?

   Share your findings as a whole class.

RESPOND

1   Fill a page with 'concrete' words – words that 'look the way they mean'. Here are a few to inspire you:

THREE BLIND MICE
THREE BLIND MICE
THREE BLIND MI

LOS^E ^{OR G}AIN
WEIGHT CENTRE

TRIPLETS
TRIPLETS
TRIPLETS
TRIPLETS

ST AC CA TO

or

2 Write your own poem entitled 'Eating Is' (or 'Sleeping Is', or ...); or
'If ... Were ...' (Substitute whatever words you wish for a poem modelled
on 'If Words Were Birds'.).
or

3 Write a poem which, like 'Bradford', relies on one word only for
its effectiveness.
or

4 Write any free verse you wish. Then go back over it to see how you might
tamper with the words to make them more concrete or visually creative
and interesting.

READ

All of these creative efforts are commonly known as concrete or shape poems.

like   attracts   like
like   attracts   like
like   attracts   like
like   attracts   like
like   attracts   like
like attracts like
like attracts like
likeattractslike
likeattractslike
likeattractslike
likeattractslike
likeattraclike
likeatlike

EMMETT WILLIAMS

MIRROR

When you look   kool uoy nehW
into a mirror   rorrim a otni
it is not   ton si ti
yourself you see,   ,ees uoy flesruoy
but a kind   dnik a tub
of apish error   rorre hsipa fo
posed in fearful   lufraef ni desop
symmetry.   .yrtemmys

JOHN UPDIKE

BEWAREOFTHESTEPLEASE
LEAVEALLBELONGINGSIN
THEFOYERLOOKOUTDEPRE
SSLEVERFORELEASEKEEP
OUTRESPASSERSHALLBEP
ROSECUTEDPUSHBARTOPE
NTHEPENALTYSHALLNOTB
ELESSTHANASCALEOFSLI
DINGINCREMENTSKEEPOF
FTHEGRASSFORGIVEUSOU
RTRESPASSESTHISMEANS
YOUISANOFFENCEPUNISH
ABLEBYDEATHNOSMOKING
BEQUIETUNSUITABLEFOR
PATRONSUNDEREIGHTEEN
YEARSOFAGEBEHANGEDBY
THENECKUNTILDEADOPEN
TOTHEPUBLICONALLDAYS
EXCEPTANDMAYGODHAVEM
ERCYONYOURSOULUNACCU
STOMEDASIAMISNOEXCUS
EKEEPOUTTHISMEANSYOU

PETER MURPHY

```
        d n
u p     d n
u p     d n
u p     d n
u p     d n
u p     d n
u p     d n
u p     d n
u p     d n
u p     d n
u p     d n
u p     d n
u p     d n
u p     d n
u p     d n
u p     d n
u p     d n
u p     d n
u p     d n
u p     d n
u p     d n
u p     d n
u p     d n
u p     d n
u p     d n
u p     d n
u p     d n
u p     d n
u p     d n
u p     d n
u p     d n
u p     d n
u p
```

ALEX SELENITSCH

ARCHIVES

```
generation upon
generation upon
generation upon
generation upon
generation upon
generation upon
generation upon
generation upon
generation upon
generation upon
generation upon
generation upon
generation upon
generation upon
generation upon
generation upon
generation upon
generation upon
generation upon
generation upon
g neration upon
g neration up  n
g nerat on up  n
g nerat  n up  n
g nerat  n  p  n
g  erat  n  p  n
g  era   n  p  n
g  era   n     n
g  er    n     n
g  r     n     n
g        n     n
g        n
g
```

EDWIN MORGAN

silencesilencesilence
silencesilencesilence
silence   silence
silencesilencesilence
silencesilencesilence

EUGEN GOMRINGER

ALLAN RIDDELL

REACT

In small groups of four to six students discuss:

1   Whether each poem has anything important to say.

2   Which poem is the cleverest and why.

RESPOND

1   In groups, list some words or objects which could be suitable subjects for pattern or concrete poems. Here are some suggestions that spring to mind, to start you off:

(a) Peace (similar treatment to 'Like Attracts Like').
(b) Other pairs of opposites, such as black and white or in and out (similar treatment to 'up/dn').
    As a group, see if you can create a shape or pattern poem from your ideas.
    or
2   Make your own collection of concrete poems.

READ

The poet himself says that the following is an odd poem. What do you think?

SMITHEREENS

I spend my days
collecting smithereens.
I find them on buses
in department stores
and on busy pavements

At restaurant tables
I pick up the leftovers
of polite conversation
At railway stations
the tearful debris
of parting lovers.

I pocket my eavesdroppings
and store them away.
I make things out of them.
Nice things, sometimes.
Sometimes odd, like this.

ROGER McGOUGH

84

REACT

In small groups of four to six students, see if you can solve the mystery. What is the poet saying? What do you think of what he says?

RESPOND

1   Still in your groups, write approximately ten statements about what you believe poetry is. You are free to say what you like, as long as you truly believe it. Call your piece 'Poetry Is'. Write it in the form of poetry if you wish. Here is a sample beginning.

POETRY IS
Saying a lot
with few words.

or

2   In your groups, write up a page of 'smithereens' – ideas, topics, incidents, newspaper clippings, comments, sensations – anything that you believe would be good 'food for poetry'. Your jottings must be based on real experiences – not the products of your imagination.

or

3   Find at least three poems that you believe grew from simple 'smithereens' experienced or collected by the poet.

or

4   Keep a list of 'smithereens' in your workbook throughout the year as subjects for your writing.

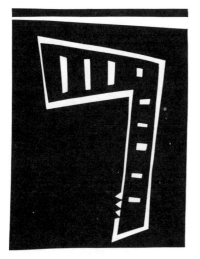

NARRATING

READ

Here is a ballad that tells the moving story of a boxer's life.

THE BALLAD OF BILLY ROSE

Outside Bristol Rovers Football Ground –
The date has gone from me, but not the day,
Nor how the dissenting flags in stiff array
Struck bravely out against the grey sky's round –

Near the Car Park then, past Austin and Ford,
Lagonda, Bentley, and a colourful patch
Of country coaches come in for the match
Was where I walked, having travelled the road

From Fishponds to watch Portsmouth in the Cup.
The Third Round, I believe. And I was filled
With the old excitement which had thrilled
Me so completely when, while growing up,

I went on Saturdays to match or fight.
Not only me; for thousands of us there
Strode forward eagerly, each man aware
Of vigorous memory, anticipating delight.

We all marched forward, all, except one man.
I saw him because he was paradoxically still,
A stone against the flood, face upright against us all,
Head bare, hoarse voice aloft. Blind as a stone.

I knew him at once despite his pathetic clothes;
Something in his stance, or his sturdy frame
Perhaps. I could even remember his name
Before I saw it on his blind-man's tray. Billy Rose.

And twenty forgetful years fell away at the sight.
Bare-kneed, dismayed, memory fled to the hub
Of Saturday violence, with friends to the Labour Club
Watching the boxing on a sawdust summer night.

The boys' enclosure close to the shabby ring
Was where we stood, clenched in a resin world,
Spoke in cool voices, lounged, were artificially bored
During minor bouts. We paid threepence to go in.

Billy Rose fought there. He was top of the bill.
So brisk a fighter, so gallant, so precise!
Trim as a tree he stood for the ceremonies,
Then turned to meet George Morgan of Tirphil.

He had no chance. Courage was not enough,
Nor tight defence. Donald Davies was sick –
We threatened his cowardice with an embarrassed kick.
Ripped across both his eyes was Rose, but we were tough

And clapped him as they wrapped his blindness up
In busy towels, applauded the wave
He gave his executioner, cheered the brave
Blind man as he cleared with a jaunty hop

The top rope. I had forgotten that day
As if it were dead for ever, yet now I saw
The flowers of punched blood on the ring floor,
As bright as his name. I do not know

How long I stood with ghosts of the wild fists
And the cries of shaken boys long dead around me,
For struck to act at last, in terror and pity
I threw some frantic money, three treacherous pence

(I cry at the memory) into his tray, and ran,
Entering the waves of the stadium like a drowning man.
Poor Billy Rose. God, he could fight
Before my three sharp coins knocked out his sight.

LESLIE NORRIS

REACT

1   Discuss, as a class, whether you agree with boxing as a sport. You may
    feel differently from one another. Give reasons for your opinions.

2   Boxing is a risky career, of course. Other jobs are risky too, though not
    always in a physical sense. Discuss, in groups of four, the pros and cons of
    the following professions:

    •   dealing on the stock exchange
    •   acting
    •   writing
    •   gambling
    •   teaching
    •   medical.

87

RESPOND

1   In pairs, write three versions of Billy Rose's career, for the following:

    •   an Old Boxers' Reunion Party
    •   a welfare worker
    •   an obituary.
    or

2   Write a short ballad about someone whose life was changed by one
    shattering event. Be careful to follow the rhyming pattern of 'The Ballad
    of Billy Rose', and write up to ten stanzas.

READ

Each of these traditional English ballads is a haunting, moving story of
love and despair. In true ballad tradition, each has a very regular rhyme
and rhythm.

THE UNQUIET GRAVE

'The wind doth blow today, my love,
And a few small drops of rain;
I never had but one true love;
In cold grave she was lain.

I'll do as much for my true love
As any young man may;
I'll sit and mourn all at her grave
For a twelvemonth and a day.'

The twelvemonth and a day being up,
The dead began to speak:
'Oh who sits weeping on my grave,
And will not let me sleep?'

''Tis I, my love, sits on your grave,
And will not let you sleep;
For I crave one kiss of your clay-cold lips
And that is all I seek.'

'You crave one kiss of my clay-cold lips;
But my breath smells earthy strong;
If you have one kiss of my clay-cold lips,
Your time will not be long.

'Tis down in yonder garden green,
Love, where we used to walk,
The finest flower that ere was seen
Is withered to a stalk.

The stalk is withered dry, my love,
So will our hearts decay;
So make yourself content, my love,
Till death calls you away.'

TRADITIONAL

A FROSTY NIGHT

'Alice, dear, what ails you,
    Dazed and lost and shaken?
Has the chill night numbed you?
    Is it fright you have taken?'

'Mother, I am very well,
    I was never better.
Mother, do not hold me so,
    Let me write my letter.'

'Sweet, my dear, what ails you?'
    'No, but I am well.
The night was cold and frosty –
    There's no more to tell.'

'Ay, the night was frosty,
    Coldly gaped the moon,
Yet the birds seemed twittering
    Through green boughs of June.

'Soft and thick the snow lay,
    Stars danced in the sky –
Not all the lambs of May-day
    Skip so bold and high.

'Your feet were dancing, Alice,
    Seemed to dance on air,
You looked a ghost or angel
    In the star-light there.

'Your eyes were frosted star-light;
    Your heart, fire and snow.
Who was it said, "I love you"?'
    'Mother, let me go!'

ROBERT GRAVES

REACT

'A FROSTY NIGHT'

1 To help us experience a poem, the poet will appeal to one or more of our five senses: sight, sound, taste, touch and smell. Which do you think is the most important sense in this poem? List all the evidence of this that you can find.

2 How would you describe the tone (see page 147) of this poem? How do you think the language used in the poem creates this tone?

3 Do you think the mother's guess was right? Is there any reason for her to come to this conclusion?

'THE UNQUIET GRAVE'

1 List all the words and phrases that contribute to the cold, desolate mood of this ballad.

2 The subject matter of this poem is wildly romantic. Do you think this sort of romance still exists today? How would a modern lover mourn?

RESPOND

1 'The Unquiet Grave' has a regular, rhythmic beat. Form a group and create a simple tune for *one* of these ballads. Indeed, *both* ballads could probably be sung to the same tune. Practise your performance and present it to the class. Concentrate on creating the haunting sound of these moving ballads.
or

2 In pairs, practise and present a dramatised performance of 'A Frosty Night'. Find ways (with props, costumes, sound effects and lighting) to create the poem's tense and dramatic tone.
or

3 (a) Write a ballad as if you were a ghost, speaking to those you loved and left behind. Use the same form as in 'The Unquiet Grave'.
or
   (b) Read again 'A Frosty Night'. Who do you think Alice is writing to? And why does she want to keep it a secret? Write the letter you imagine Alice is trying to write in the poem.

READ

In 1934 there was an explosion in the Gresford pit in Denbighshire, North Wales. The victims of this twentieth century tragedy are remembered in the following poem.

THE GRESFORD DISASTER

You've heard of the Gresford disaster,
The terrible price that was paid,
Two hundred and forty-two colliers were lost
And three men of a rescue brigade.

It occurred in the month of September,
At three in the morning, that pit
Was racked by a violent explosion
In the Dennis where gas lay so thick.

The gas in the Dennis deep section
Was packed there like snow in a drift,
And many a man had to leave the coal-face
Before he had worked out his shift.

A fortnight before the explosion,
To the shot-firer Tomlinson cried
'If you fire that shot we'll be all blown to hell!'
And no one can say that he lied.

The fireman's reports they are missing
The records of forty-two days;
The colliery manager had them destroyed
To cover his criminal ways.

Down there in the dark they are lying,
They died for nine shillings a day.
They have worked out their shift and now they must lie
In the darkness until Judgement Day.

The Lord Mayor of London's collecting
To help both our children and wives,
The owners have sent some white lilies
To pay for the poor colliers' lives.

Farewell, our dear wives and our children.
Farewell, our old comrades as well.
Don't send your sons down the dark dreary pit.
They'll be damned like the sinners in hell.

TRADITIONAL

92

REACT

In small groups, 'translate' this poem into a prose account of the disaster.
You will need to decide on the content of your paragraphs, as one stanza will
not necessarily 'translate' to one prose paragraph. While you can make your
prose version as dramatic as you like in style – that is, in the way you report it
– you need to be accurate about the factual content of the poem.

RESPOND

1 Natural disasters, and those caused by humans, are unfortunately a fact
   of life. Here are some photographs of modern disasters. Write a prose or
   poetry account of one of these disasters, or of an even more current
   catastrophe that you can remember.
   or

2 In your workbook, paste a cutting that reports a particular tragedy or
   disaster. Jot down your random reactions on reading of the event. You
   might like to use these in your writing later on.

• **O**n January 29, 1986, seventy-three seconds after lift-off from Florida's Cape Canaveral, the space shuttle Challenger exploded. Its crew of five men and two women died, including the first civilian to go into space, school teacher Christa McAuliffe.

• **T**en minutes before a match, when the gates were opened to allow Liverpool fans into Sheffield's Hillsborough stadium, ninety-six people were crushed to death or asphyxiated and one hundred and seventy were seriously injured.

• Bushfires scorched an 800-kilometre-long trail of horror, panic and death through drought-stricken Victoria and South Australia in February, 1983. They were the worst bushfires in Australian history: seventy-two died, and eight thousand were left homeless.

READ

This is a most unusual contemporary narrative poem with quite a lot to say.

INTERRUPTION AT THE OPERA HOUSE

At the very beginning of an important symphony,
while the rich and famous were settling into their quietly expensive boxes,
a man came crashing through the crowds,
carrying in his hand a cage in which
the rightful owner of the music sat,
yellow and tiny and very poor;
and taking onto the rostrum this rather timid bird
he turned up the microphones, and it sang.

'A very original beginning to the evening,' said the crowds,
quietly glancing at their programmes to find
the significance of the intrusion.

Meanwhile at the box office, the organisers of the evening
were arranging for small and uniformed attendants
to evict, even forcefully, the intruders.
But as the attendants, poor and gathered from the nearby slums at little expense,
went rushing down the aisles to do their job
they heard above the coughing and irritable rattling of jewels,
a sound that filled their heads with light,
and from somewhere inside them there bubbled up a stream,
and there came a breeze on which their youth was carried.
How sweetly the bird sang!

And though soon the fur-wrapped crowds
were leaving their boxes and in confusion were winding their way home
still the attendants sat in the aisles,
and some, so delighted at what they heard, rushed out to call
their families and friends.

And their children came,
sleepy for it was late in the evening,
very late in the evening,
and they hardly knew if they had done with dreaming
or had begun again.
In all the tenement blocks
the lights were clicking on,
and the rightful owner of the music,
tiny and no longer timid, sang
for the rightful owners of the song.

BRIAN PATTEN

REACT

Sit in one large circle to read and talk about this poem. Here are some
possible discussion questions.

1   What does the poet mean by calling the bird the 'rightful owner of the
    music' and the poor people the 'rightful owners of the song'?

2   How does the poet feel about the original symphony audience? Use
    words and phrases from the poem to back up your argument.

3   The first two verses have a contrast between quiet and noise. Do you
    think the poet has done this deliberately?

4   This is what is sometimes called a 'prose poem', because it has the
    rhythms of conversational prose. What effect does this conversational
    rhythm have on the meaning?

RESPOND

1   Write a well-structured paragraph (with an introductory sentence, a
    number of explanatory sentences and a concluding sentence) giving your
    thoughts on this poem's message or theme.
    or
2   Write your own prose poem, with conversational rhythms, to criticise
    indirectly something which you think is unfair.

DESCRIBING

READ
Each of these two poems captures the breathless excitement of a
'magic moment'.

OUT OF SCHOOL

Four o'clock strikes,
There's a rising hum,
Then the doors fly open,
The children come.

With a wild cat-call
And a hop-scotch hop
And a bouncing ball
And a whirling top.

Grazing of knees,
A hair-pull and a slap,
A hitched-up satchel,
A pulled down cap,

Bully boys reeling off,
Hurt ones squealing off,
Aviators wheeling off,
Mousy ones stealing off,

Woollen gloves for chilblains,
Cotton rags for snufflers,
Pigtails, coat-tails,
Tails of mufflers,

Machine-gun cries,
A kennelful of snarlings,
A hurricane of leaves,
A treeful of starlings,

Thinning away now
By some and some,
Thinning away, away,
All gone home.

HAL SUMMERS

97

AT THE MATCH.
HARRY'S MONOLOGUE

HARRY: Come Saturday,
The whole town comes alive.
People are going one way,
From all the streets,
They are going the one way,
And meeting and joining,
And going on and meeting more and more
Till the trickle becomes a flood.
And men are packed so tight
That cars have to nose their way through.
And you come to the stadium,
And it's humming,
A hum comes from the bowl.
And the people inside seem to be saying,
Come on in, come on in,
And you jostle at the turnstile,
And the turnstile clicks and clicks,
And push nearer and nearer,
Through the dark gap,
Then you're in.
And the great stand of the City End,
It's like a hall,
A great hall,
And you go on,
Through the arch
And you see the pitch,
Green, new shaven and watered,
And the groundsman's made the white lines,
As straight as a ruler,
And the ash is pressed.
And you find your place among the fans,
The real fans,
The singers and chanters and rattle wavers.
And a sheet of tobacco smoke hangs over the crowd.
And the crowd whistles and hoots,
And the policemen circling the pitch
Look up and know they're in for a rough day of it,
And the stadium fills up,
The Open End first, then the City End,
Then the paddock, then the covered seated stand,
Then, last of all, the fat directors
With the Lord Mayor and cigars.

And the reporters are in their little glass box,

And the cameramen position themselves

By the goal,

And there's a looking down the tunnel,

Then a hush.

Then out they come.

The lads,

Like toy footballers on a green billiard table.

And the roar goes up ...

PETER TERSON

REACT

1   Divide the class into two groups. One group is to write 'At the Match' in prose form; whilst the other group does the same with 'Out of School'. You could work as groups on this activity if you like – with one person acting as a scribe for each group – or you might choose to do the activity as individuals. Whatever you choose, don't add or subtract any content for your prose version. You will only need to change sentence structure (and perhaps add connecting words) to make your prose version sound like connected, natural prose.

When you have done this, read the prose versions to the whole class. Which sounds better in each case – the prose version or the poetry version? What, if anything, is achieved in the poetry version that wasn't achieved in the prose version?

2   What is similar about the ways in which these two poems develop?

3   Which of the five senses does each poet use in the poem's imagery?

RESPOND

1   Write your own poem about a particular event. Events like the following would lend themselves to the free verse form of 'At the Match':
   • any sporting event;
   • parades or processions;
   • celebrations;
   • a pop or orchestral concert;
   • any event that builds up to a grand opening, climax or finale.
Events like those listed below might lend themselves more to the shorter, sharper, more energetic form of 'Out of School':
   • a sale or auction;
   • a dance;
   • the peak hour;
   • any 'frantic' time or occasion.
or

2 In pairs *or* as individuals, write some action poetry in response to one of these photographs. (You may choose to write about the events leading up to or surrounding the photograph rather than about the actual photograph itself.)

READ

Each of these 'creature poems' well captures the natures of the creatures
depicted – the wild dog, the quaintly plodding emus, the contented cows and
the shadowy worms.

LONE DOG

I'm a lean dog, a keen dog, a wild dog, and lone;
I'm a rough dog, a tough dog, hunting on my own;
I'm a bad dog, a mad dog, teasing silly sheep;
I love to sit and bay the moon, to keep fat souls from sleep.

I'll never be a lap dog, licking dirty feet,
A sleek dog, a meek dog, cringing for my meat,
Not for me the fireside, the well-filled plate,
But shut door, and sharp stone, and cuff, and kick, and hate.

Not for me the other dogs, running by my side,
Some have run a short while, but none of them would bide,
O mine is still the lone trail, the hard trail, the best,
Wild wind, and wild stars, and the hunger of the quest!

IRENE R. McLEOD

EMUS

It is
particularly
the particular way
they come
stepping
warily
along the path
in dark
wrinkled
stockings
and shabby
mini fur coats,
their weaving
Donald Duck
heads
ready
to dip
and snatch
your ice cream
that appeals;
that,
and the way
they browse dumbly brown
in cattle-paddocks.

CHRIS WALLACE-CRABBE

102

COWS

Half the time they munched the grass,
    and all the time they lay
Down in the water-meadows, the lazy month
    of May,
       A-chewing,
       A-mooing,
    To pass the time away.
    Nice weather,
           said the brown cow.
 Ah,
    said the white.
Grass is very tasty.
Grass is all right.

Half the time they munched the grass,
    and all the time they lay
Down in the water-meadows, the lazy month
    of May,
      A-chewing,
      A-mooing,
    To pass the time away.
    Rain coming,
          said the brown cow.
  Ah,
    said the white.
  Flies is very tiresome.
  Flies bite.

Half the time they munched the grass,
    and all the time they lay
Down in the water-meadows, the lazy month
    of May,
      A-chewing,
      A-mooing,
    To pass the time away.
    Time to go,
          said the brown cow.
  Ah,
    said the white.
  Nice chat.
  Very pleasant.
  Night.
  Night.

Half the time they munched the grass,
    and half the time they lay
Down in the water-meadows, the lazy month
    of May,
      A-chewing,
      A-mooing,
    To pass the time away.

JAMES REEVES

WORMS AND THE WIND

Worms would rather be worms.

Ask a worm and he says, 'Who knows what a worm knows?'

Worms go down and up and over and under.

Worms like tunnels.

When worms talk they talk about the worm world.

Worms like it in the dark.

Neither the sun nor the moon interests a worm.

Zigzag worms hate circle worms.

Curve worms never trust square worms.

Worms know what worms want.

Slide worms are suspicious of crawl worms.

One worm asks another, 'How does your belly drag today?'

The shape of a crooked worm satisfies a crooked worm.

A straight worm says, 'Why not be straight?'

Worms tired of crawling begin to slither.

Long worms slither farther than short worms.

Middle-sized worms say, 'It is nice to be neither long nor short.'

Old worms teach young worms to say, 'Don't be sorry for me unless you have been a
    worm and lived in worm places and read worm books.'

When worms go to war they dig in, come out and fight, dig in again, come out and fight
    again, dig in again, and so on.

Worms underground never hear the wind overground and sometimes they ask, 'What is
    this wind we hear of?'

CARL SANDBURG

REACT

In small groups of four to six students, discuss each of these poems.

'LONE DOG'

How do rhyme, rhythm and alliteration help to create the picture and the
feeling of a fearless, rugged wild dog in 'Lone Dog'?

    While there is certainly a lot of end rhyme (rhyme at the ends of lines)
in this poem, look too at the poem's internal rhyme – that is, rhymes within
a line, such as 'a *lean* dog, a *keen* dog'. What effect do these have on
the rhythm?

    As you discuss the poem, be sure to read the lines aloud. Only in this way
will you notice the full effect of the rhyme, rhythm and alliteration.

'COWS'

How do the rhyme, rhythm, repetition and form help to create the mood or
atmosphere of 'Cows'?

Before you start your discussion, call for three volunteers to read the poem aloud – one to read the part of narrator, the other two to read the parts of the conversing cows.

'EMUS'

Discuss the relevance of the form or shape of 'Emus'. Read this poem aloud, too. Does the form help create the character and nature of the emus?

What do you think of the poem's two metaphors? What is the effect of the image in the second last line?

'WORMS AND THE WIND'

This poem has a most unusual subject. Read it aloud first, paying special attention to the pauses which help create the poem's mood. Try to reach some agreement on these issues as a group:

(a) Is it an appealing poem?
(b) Is it a good poem? (Discuss here whether its form and feeling are appropriate to its topic.)
(c) What is the effect of the repetition of the words 'worms' and 'worm'?

Share your findings as a class. Each class member could then write an appreciation or review of their favourite poem of the four, outlining the issues discussed.

RESPOND

As a whole class, discuss what other creatures would suit each of the forms above. What other creatures, for example, could be considered 'worm-like' and might suit the matter-of-fact tone and prosaic (like prose) rhythm of 'Worms and the Wind'? What others could be considered fierce and harsh, like the 'Lone Dog'; quaint and awkward like the emus; or contented and lazy like the cows?

Now write your own animal poem, making your poem in some way echo the nature and 'personality' of the animal you choose, just as the above poems have done. One of these photographs may help to inspire you.

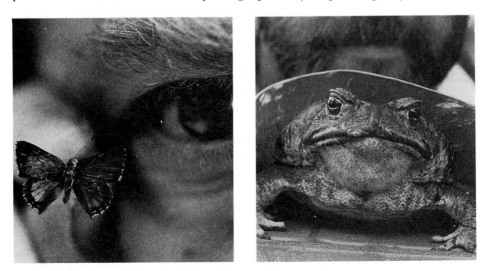

READ

Here we have two poems about two very different workers: a postman and a
farmer. Each poem, in its own way, shows the simple power and importance
of these occupations.

THE POSTMAN

Satchel on hip
the postman goes
from doorstep to doorstep
and stooping sows

each letterbox
with seed. His right
hand all the morning makes
the same half circle. White

seed he scatters,
a fistful of
featureless letters
pregnant with ruin or love.

I watch him zig-
zag down the street
dipping his hand in that big
bag, sowing the cool, neat

envelopes which
make *twenty-one*
unaccountably rich,
twenty-two an orphan.

I cannot see
them but I know
others are watching. We
stoop in a row

(as he turns away),
straighten and stand
weighing and delaying
the future in one hand.

JON STALLWORTHY

FROM 'TOM FARLEY'

Tom Farley, up to his knees in sheep
By the drafting yard, moves in a red fog
Of summer dust; moves, bent, in a rhythm deep
As the seasons, his hard-soft hands
Holding gentle conversation with his dog.

Tom Farley on his Mid-North run
Has a face as fresh and kindly as his sheep;
Wears an old felt hat with its brim full of sun,
Sees the waves of wool move as soothingly as sleep.

COLIN THIELE

REACT

As a whole class, discuss these points:

1   What power does the postman seem to have? What simple metaphor does
the poet use to explain this power?

2   Colin Thiele seems to capture Tom Farley's basic goodness and
dedication. How does the language of the poem convey this?

3   As individuals, choose what you consider to be the most important lines
in 'The Postman' and the most effective image in 'Tom Farley'.

Share your thoughts as a whole class.

RESPOND

1   Write a piece of prose or poetry about another occupation that may seem ordinary enough, but which is 'powerful' in its own way.

    or

2   In a piece of prose entitled 'On My Rounds', capture the thoughts of either Tom Farley or the postman as they go about their daily work. This sentence may help to set the mood for you:

    'Geez, it's hot today. No matter, here we go ...'

READ

'The Spider' seems quite artless and simple on first reading.

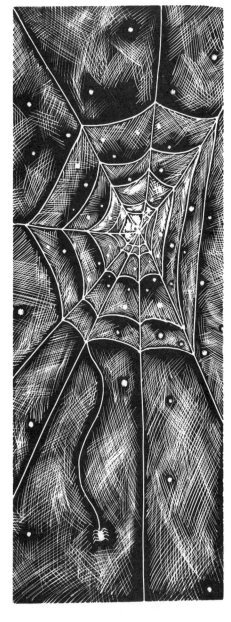

THE SPIDER

The spider fishes the air with its net
Where the flies and insects go past;
Its web is fine as lines of a fingerprint
Or scratches on a pane of glass.

Round as a ball of string,
With silken ladders stretching
Out from the centre where it is sitting,
It walks on air in every direction.

It stitches up a hole
In the empty air
Or hangs on its own rope,
When its web is broken, to make a repair.

A spider is a miniature monster
That draws its web on a shadow
High up in a dusty corner
Or comes in the house and curtains the window.

Outside on a misty morning the trap it spreads
Catches dew instead of flies
And the sun picks pearls from the threads
As they gradually dry.

And in the winter the scores of webs
Have nothing left to catch
In the leafless hedge
But the breath of the frost.

STANLEY COOK

REACT

In pairs, explore the poem more closely. It is actually a very artful poem with words and images carefully chosen. What poetic 'gems', of language or imagery, can you find?

Share your findings as a whole class.

RESPOND

Hold a poem-sharing session which you call 'Simply Clever'. Each student is to find and contribute one descriptive poem – one which is simple and appealing yet cleverly conceived.

You may choose to make a wall-chart of your poem with comments that pin-point the poetic gems, or you may prefer to make an overhead transparency of your poem and discuss it orally with the class.

Any presentation method at all will do – as long as it enables you to share your choice.

READ

'African Beggar' is a strikingly realistic poem. Read it together and note the poet's harsh and carefully chosen descriptions.

AFRICAN BEGGAR

Sprawled in the dust outside the Syrian store,
a target for small children, dogs and flies,
a heap of verminous rags and matted hair,
he watches us with cunning, reptile eyes,
his noseless, smallpoxed face creased in a sneer.

Sometimes he shows his yellow stumps of teeth
and whines for alms, perceiving that we bear
the curse of pity; a grotesque mask of death,
with hands like claws about his begging-bowl.

But often he is lying all alone
within the shadow of a crumbling wall,
lost in the trackless jungle of his pain,
clutching the pitiless red earth in vain
and whimpering like a stricken animal.

RAYMOND TONG

REACT

Divide into groups of four to six students to discuss the poet's word pictures or imagery. Often images are created simply through an unexpected choice of descriptive words. Sometimes, though, images are created by using metaphors (see page 147). In line 3 of 'African Beggar', for example, the poet does not see the beggar as a person, but as 'a heap of verminous rags and matted hair'.

Sometimes, too, the poet uses a comparison to help create an image. In the last line, for example, the beggar whimpers 'like a stricken animal'. This kind of comparison is called a *simile* (see page 147).

• In your small groups, explore the poet's choice of words and use of similes and metaphors. Choose one person from each group to make a statement on these points to the whole class.

RESPOND

Choose one of the following activities.

1   Check current newspapers for advertisements seeking sponsors and/or support for the poor in Third World countries. Find other students who are willing to contribute to such a scheme. Collect the appropriate funds and together write a covering letter to send to the agency.
     or

2   Write about our world of contrasts, which breeds both wealth and poverty. One of these titles may inspire you:
     • A pitiless world.
     • From rags to riches.
     • It could be me...
     or

3   Use these questions as the basis for some research into poverty in Africa.
     • What contributes to the poverty there? Race? Overpopulation? Economy?
     • What measures are being taken to alleviate poverty in Africa?
     Read your report to the whole class.

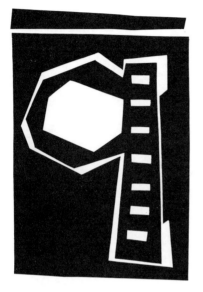

CRITICISING

READ

Here we have a variety of poems about various ideas and issues of today.
Read and enjoy them together.

THE PLAYGROUND

In the playground
At the back of our house
There have been some changes.

They said the climbing frame was
NOT SAFE
So they sawed it down.

They said the paddling pool was
NOT SAFE
So they drained it dry.

They said the see-saw was
NOT SAFE
So they took it away.

They said the sandpit was
NOT SAFE
So they fenced it in.

They said the playground was
NOT SAFE
So they locked it up.

Sawn down
Drained dry
Taken away
Fenced in
Locked up

How do you feel?
Safe?

MICHAEL ROSEN

IT IS IMPOSSIBLE

It is impossible
for anyone to enter
our small world.
The adults don't
understand us
they think
we're childish.
No-one can get in
our world
It has a wall twenty feet high
and adults
Have only ten-feet ladders.

ROSS FALCONER

ELEGY TO MYSELF

Never ask who i am
i am page 7 of the newspaper
or the part between commercials
or 6 o'clock, 10 o'clock, 11 o'clock
i am the mother who doesn't know
where her children are
i am Belfast blood, Boston blood, Brooklyn blood
i am a cop, a college girl, a storekeeper
or an Olympic athlete
i am an elderly woman afraid to leave my house
a bird in a gilded cage
i am a passer-by, i, too, am a victim
robbed, mugged, harassed, knifed, raped, beaten
kidnapped, dead instantly, dead on arrival
or much later
never ask who i am
the paragraphs in the paper are always there
inevitably
the names are always your name.

DINA GRUSSGOTT

113

GOODWILL TO MEN, GIVE US YOUR MONEY

It was Christmas Eve on a Friday,
    The shops were full of cheer,
With tinsel in the windows,
    And presents twice as dear.
A thousand Father Christmases
    Sat in their little huts,
And folks was buying crackers,
    And folks was buying nuts.

All up and down the country,
    Before the light was snuffed,
Turkeys they got murdered,
    And cockerels they got stuffed,
Christmas cakes got marzipanned,
    And puddin's they got steamed,
Mothers they got desperate,
    And tired kiddies screamed.

Hundredweights of Christmas cards
    Went flying through the post,
With first-class postage stamps on those
    You had to flatter most.
Within a million kitchens,
    Mince pies was being made.
On everybody's radio,
    'White Christmas' it was played.

Out in the frozen countryside,
    Men crept round on their own,
Hacking off the holly
    What other folks had grown,
Mistletoe in willow trees
    Was by a man wrenched clear,
So he could kiss his neighbour's wife,
    He'd fancied all the year.

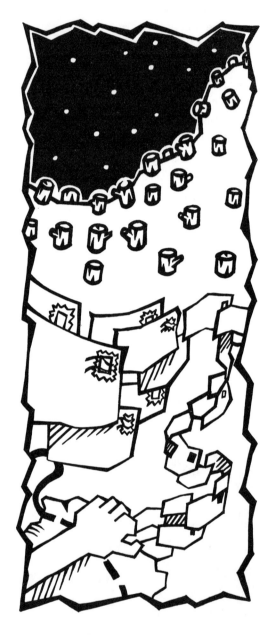

And out upon the hillside,
      Where the Christmas trees had stood,
All was completely barren,
      But for little stumps of wood.
The little trees that flourished
      All the year were there no more,
But in a million houses,
      Dropped their needles on the floor.

And out of every cranny, cupboard,
      Hiding place and nook,
Little bikes and kiddies' trikes,
      Were secretively took.
Yards of wrapping paper,
      Was rustled round about,
And bikes where wheeled to bedrooms,
      With the pedals sticking out.

Rolled up in Christmas paper,
      The Action Men were tensed,
All ready for the morning,
      When their fighting life commenced.
With tommy guns and daggers,
      All clustered round about,
'Peace on Earth – Goodwill to Men',
      The figures seemed to shout.

The church was standing empty,
      The pub was standing packed,
There came a yell, 'Noel, Noel!'
      And glasses they got cracked.
From up above the fireplace,
      Christmas cards began to fall,
And trodden on the floor, said:
      'Merry Xmas to you all'.

PAM AYRES

115

HOOLIGANISM

Ten little football fans
Making rude signs,
One swore at a policeman
Then there were nine.

Nine little football fans
Stirring up some hate,
One got bottled
and then there were eight.

Eight little football fans,
The youngest was eleven,
He smashed up a buffet
And then there were seven.

Seven little football fans
Hitting people with sticks,
One tried to fight alone
Then there were six.

Six little football fans
Playing with a knife,
One got stabbed
And then there were five.

Five little football fans,
One fell on the floor,
He got crushed
And then there were four.

Four little football fans,
Just like you and me,
One threw a penny at the goalie
Then there were three.

Three little football fans
The other team did boo,
But the fans outnumbered them
And then there were two.

Two little football fans,
After all was done,
One ran on the football pitch
Then there was one.

One little football fan,
Glad his team had won,
Argued with some other fans
Then there were none.

PETER KETT

COUNTING THE MAD

This one was put in a jacket,
This one was sent home,
This one was given bread and meat
But would eat none,
And this one cried No No No No
All day long.

This one looked at the window
As though it were a wall,
This one saw things that were not there,
This one things that were,
And this one cried No No No No
All day long.

This one thought himself a bird,
This one a dog.
And this one thought himself a man,
An ordinary man,
And cried and cried No No No No
All day long.

DONALD JUSTICE

117

REACT

1   In groups of four to six students, match each poem to *one* of these
    themes:
    • Christmas has lost its true meaning and spirit.
    • Lack of communication.
    • The negative side of sport.
    • *All* people, no matter who, should be treated as individuals.

- To feel safe, we must also feel free.
- We are all a part of each other's suffering.

2 Discuss how each poet explores his or her theme. Decide:
  - if what the poet says is original;
  - if the poem has made you think about the issue for the first time;
  - if the message is important;
  - if the poem itself (its form, use of language, etc.) is unusual or striking.

3 By yourself, write about three of the poems. Explain:
  - the poem's theme – in your own words;
  - your thoughts on, or reactions to, this theme;
  - your assessment of the writer's craft – of how the poem is written.

RESPOND

1 Write about three paragraphs expressing your views on one of the following:
  - Sport
  - Christmas
  - The 'Communication Gap'
  - Caring for a particular group of underprivileged people.

or

2 Look carefully at the form or structure of 'The Playground'. Note:
  - how the first verse 'sets the scene';
  - the pattern repeated in each of the next five verses;
  - the next verse which summarises all the evils mentioned in the previous five verses;
  - the last two lines which very subtly drive home a message.

Model your own 'message poem' on this structure. Some of these phrases may give you some ideas:

In our house
Around here
At our school   } to set the scene?
Wherever I look
NOT SUITABLE
NOT OLD ENOUGH
NOT POSSIBLE   } as the repeated line?
NOT WANTED
NOT RESPONSIBLE

or

3 (a) Respond creatively to 'Elegy to Myself'. (An elegy is a song or lament for the dead.) Use artwork, press clippings, photographs, other poems – anything that this poem inspires.

(b) Alternatively, you may wish to write a similar poem referring to the more immediate issues of today. Use the photograph as a starting point if you like.

READ

These two poems explore the issue of poverty in different ways. Both the poems are ironical, that is, while they say one thing, they really mean something else – their intention is to mock.

THE COMMISSION

In this poem their is a table
Groaning with food.
There is also a child
Groaning for lack of food.
The food is beautifully photographed
The meat more succulent
The fruit as juicy
As you are likely to see.
(The child is sketched in lightly
She is not important.)
The photograph is to be used
In a glossy magazine
As part of a campaign
Advertising after-dinner mints.

This evening the photographer
In receipt of his fee
Celebrates by dining with friends
In a famous West End restaurant.
Doodling on the napkin between courses
The photographer, always creative,
Draws a little Asian girl,
Naked, wide-eyed, pleading.
The photographer is pleased.
He has an idea for the next commission,
The one for famine relief.
The tandoori arrives
He puts away his pen
And picks up a fork.

ROGER McGOUGH

120

THE APPEAL

Don't give them your money.
They don't really need it.
It'll only create problems.
We need helpless people
and money wipes them out.
Too much food
and they'll have to
bring in the slimming pills.
Too much success
and they'll have to
fly in psychiatrists.
These folk have found the simple life,
the open-air life, the life
unencumbered by possessions,
by status.
Don't export the
curse of affluence
to the Third World.
They'll only become like us
or, if we give too freely,
we'll become like them.

STEVE TURNER

REACT

'THE APPEAL'

In groups of four to six, decide which is the truest statement in each of the following groups. Before you start your discussion, be sure you understand what is meant by:

* unencumbered
* status
* affluence
* Third World.

Statements

1   The poet is:
    (a) saying something about the evil of money and success;
    (b) saying that there are benefits in living in the Third World;
    (c) expressing both of these ideas.

2   The poet:
    (a) is afraid that we will become poor if we give too much away;
    (b) believes that dealing with poverty is a difficult task;
    (c) really believes – despite what he appears to be saying – that we should help the poor.

'THE COMMISSION'

Again in your small groups, decide whether each of these statements is true or false. Before you start, be sure to check that you know the meaning of:

* succulent
* commission
* tandoori.

Statements

1   The poet believes that we are too pre-occupied with our own concerns to really appreciate what others feel or suffer.
2   The photographer is a selfish person.
3   The photographer does not realise that there is anything wrong with what he is doing.
4   We cannot be blamed for our heartlessness when we don't really experience hardship ourselves.
5   Such poems are cruel and pointless.

RESPOND

1   Write a prose passage entitled 'Poverty', including any thoughts and feelings inspired by either or both of these poems.

    or

2   Write some poetry about any aspect of poverty. Here is one student's poem which may give you extra inspiration:

THE POOR

Huddled in ancient rags,
Shadows of pity,
Timeless, though worn by time,
They have no life
The streets are their world.

They know not
Of the statues of power
Suited to lying.
They are rigid;
They do not give.

The stars are their only treasures,
Those of the heart.
Hope
For a few more crumbs.

They stare with glazed eyes,
Under cover of the night
At the rich surrounding them
Who shiver with horror
At the sick zombies they are.

'Pretty, rich'
Their thoughts a jumble:
An eternal machine generating images
Of the brilliant, effervescent gods
As they go by.

When they are gone
The poor return to
Their benches, corners, alleys
And dream their fantasy
Of food, the rich,
The gods' lives.

But by morning
The images are gone
Away to the dream-box.
Another sunrise, another day.

What is there to live for?
Tomorrow?
Merely an extension of today ...
Without hope.

ALEX TAIT (student)

READ

This poet pours out his beliefs and opinions in one hard-hitting 'outburst'.

I AM ON THE KIDS' SIDE

I am on the kids' side
in the war against adults.
I don't want to stand still.
I don't want to sit still.
I don't want to be quiet.
I believe that strangers
are for staring at,
bags are for looking into,
paper is for scribbling on.
I want to know Why.
I want to know How.
I wonder What If.
I am on the kids' side
in the war against tedium.
I'm for going home
when stores get packed.
I'm for sleeping in
when parties get dull.
I'm for kicking stones
when conversation sags.
I'm for making noises.
I'm for playing jokes –
especially in life's
more Serious Bits.
I am on the kids' side.
See my sneaky grin,
watch me dance, see me run.
Spit on the carpet, rub it in,
pick my nose in public,
play rock stars in the mirror.

I am on the kids' side.
I want to know why we're not moving.
I'm fed up. I want to go out.
What's that? Can I have one?
It isn't fair. Who's that man?
It wasn't me, I was pushed.
When are we going to go?
I am on the kids' side
putting fun back into words.
Ink pink pen and ink
you go out because you stink.
Stephen Turner is a burner,
urner, murner, purner.
Stephen, weven, peven,
reven, teven, Turnip Top.
I am on the kids' side
in the war against apathy.
Mum, I want to do something.
It must be my turn next.
When can we go out?
I am on the kids' side
and when I grow up,
I want to be a boy.

STEVE TURNER

REACT

Hold a panel discussion of this poem. Here are some guidelines.

1   Read the poem as a whole class, then take a little time to become familiar
    with it as individuals.

2   Five students then volunteer to form the panel and sit at the front
    of the room.

3   Each panel member in turn gives her or his reactions to the poem. The
    audience listens carefully so that they can challenge or question
    individual speakers at the end of the panelists' contributions.

4   After the proceedings, the class audience (not the panel members) write
    up a 'Reaction Report' on the poem.

RESPOND

1 Write your vigorous support for someone or something in a similar way.
  For example:
  I am on the animals' side
  in the war against man.
  or
2 Find two or more poems which, like this one, have the rhythms of speech.
  Say if you think this kind of rhythm suits the poems' subjects.

READ

Each of these poems was written in response to racial or cultural prejudices.

A BLACK MAN'S SONG

I looked in the mirror.
What did I see?
Not black not white,
but me, only me.
       Coal black face
       with big bright eyes
       and lily white teeth
       that's lil old me.
Yes I looked in the mirror.
What did I see?
I saw a fella
who's dear to me.
       Short broad nose,
       full thick lips
       and black kinky hair;
       man that's me.
Oh I looked in the mirror.
What did I see?
I saw a fella
as cute as can be,
       that must be me.
If you look
in the mirror,
what will you see?
       You may see black,
       you may see white;
       but you won't see me,
       no siree not me.

JIMI RAND

THIS ENGLAND?

...guests at midnight
                                    stopping
outside the house. The one
without the gun demands

her name and (through
and interpreter) tells Mammie

she's got nothing to fear
if she's legal.

E. A. MARKHAM

CIVILISATION

We who came late to civilisation,
Missing a gap of centuries,
When you came we marvelled and admired,
But with foreboding.
We had so little but we had happiness,
Each day a holiday,
For we were people before we were citizens,
Before we were ratepayers,
Tenants, customers, employees, parishioners.
How could we understand
White man's gradings, rigid and unquestioned,
Your sacred totems of Lord and Lady,
Highness and Holiness, Eminence, Majesty.
We could not understand
Your strange cult of uniformity,
This mass obedience to clocks, time-tables.
Puzzled, we wondered why
The importance to you, urgent and essential,
Of ties and gloves, shoe-polish, uniforms.

New to us were jails and orphanages,
Rents and taxes, banks and mortgages.
We who had so few things, the prime things,
We had no policemen, lawyers, middlemen,
Brokers, financiers, millionaires.
So they bewildered us, all the new wonders,
Stocks and shares, real estate,
Compound interest, sales and investments.
Oh, we have benefited, we have been lifted
With new knowledge, a new world opened.
Suddenly caught up in white man ways
Gladly and gratefully we accept,
And this is necessity.
But remember, white man, if life is for happiness,
You too, surely, have much to change.

OODGEROO NOONUCCAL (Kath Walker)

FROM MAMA DOT

Born on a sunday
in the kingdom of Ashante

Sold on a monday
into slavery

Ran away on tuesday
cause she born free

Lost a foot on wednesday
when they catch she

Worked all thursday
till her head grey

Dropped on friday
where they burned she

Freed on saturday
in a new century

FRED D'AGUIAR

REACT

Select at random a 'buzz group' of a quarter of the students in the class. They go to the front of the room (or anywhere where the rest of the class can act as an audience) to react spontaneously to one of these poems. Repeat the process with a new buzz group for each of the four poems.

Follow these guidelines:

1   Start with short, spontaneous responses, as in brainstorming. Let the discussion develop more seriously from these initial comments. About five minutes should be enough time to discuss each poem.

2   The audience is then free to add to (or comment on) what has been raised in the buzz group.

3   To ensure that the whole class is involved in reacting to the poem decide, as a class, which line or lines in each poem could be said to best sum up that poem's theme. Do this for each poem on conclusion of the buzz group's discussion.

RESPOND

1   In pairs, write a poem taking 'A Black Man's Song' as a model. Write one verse each until you've finished. You can bring in a racial or a cultural prejudice – whichever you know the most about

    or

2   Using 'This England' as a starting point, write a short poem about one aspect of racial prejudice – something you have either experienced or witnessed.

REFLECTING

READ

'Evening' is an arresting poem, with very carefully chosen language and a skilfully contrived form.

EVENING

The visitors are gone and an empty wind
Loiters in the picnic ground. A pensive bird
Stands on long legs in the darkening water;
The road beckons nobody, and loneliness
Wafts like fog among the grim trees.
                              In the wards
The evening meal is over, the TV sets
Flick on. Old folk palpitate in corners
Waiting for night when they will sleep or die.

PETER KOCAN

REACT

In groups of four to six, explore these aspects of 'Evening'.

1   List all the words which you feel contribute to the poem's empty, despondent mood.

2   Discuss the effectiveness of:
    ... loneliness
    Wafts like fog among the grim trees.

3   What is the effect of the last line? What causes this effect?

4   Why do you suppose the poet placed the line 'In the wards' as he did?

5   Poets are extremely careful about the shaping of their lines into a particular form; they are extremely careful about where they break off one line and start another. Read the poem aloud again to hear where the stresses fall. Can you see any pattern of breaks here? Are certain words more effective because they occur at the beginnings of lines?

6   As a group, choose another title for the poem. You will probably need quite a bit of discussion before the group reaches agreement.

RESPOND

As a group, choose another institution which you feel you could write about: a crèche, a school, a hospital ward, an orphanage etc. (It would be even better, of course, if you could visit the institution and so write from actual experience; otherwise, imagination will have to suffice.)

   Use these guidelines to help you write a group poem about the institution you have chosen:

1   Brainstorm your ideas and images. When brainstorming, you should freely associate and suggest words, phrases, ideas, images; anything that comes into your mind (about the topic) is to be recorded. No-one is allowed to censor anything that is said at this initial stage of the writing process. Use a large sheet of paper to record all comments and suggestions. Let your ideas grow and flow from each other freely and creatively. You may be surprised at what you are able to generate in this way.

2   Put up the sheet so that all group members can see the result. Tick all the words and phrases that you think you could use in a poem. (Don't cross out anything at this stage – you may change your mind!)

3   Order the words and phrases so that they make some sort of sense as a poem.

4   Edit the result. In other words, play around with it until you are sure that you have the best words in the best order. Be especially careful – as the poet of 'Evening' was – to start and end lines at appropriate times. Try to make the last line have an impact in some way.

Continue the editing and discussion process until you are happy with the result.

5   Decide on a suitable title for your poem.

READ

We all spend a lot of time reflecting on other people, on what 'makes them tick', on why they are what they are, or why they do what they do. Each of the next three poems is reflective in this way; each gives a portrait of people in particular circumstances.

FARM CHILD

Look at this village boy, his head is stuffed
With all the nests he knows, his pockets with flowers,
Snail-shells and bits of glass, the fruit of hours
Spent in the fields by thorn and thistle tuft.
Look at his eyes, see the harebell hiding there:
Mark how the sun has freckled his smooth face
Like a finch's egg under that bush of hair
That dares the wind, and in the mixen now
Notice his poise; from such unconscious grace
Earth breeds and beckons to the stubborn plough.

R. S. THOMAS

THE PARK BENCH

Old friends,
Old friends
Sat on their park bench
Like bookends,
Surrounding emptiness.

For years,
So many years
They had stared just like this
At each other,
At nothing.

So well,
So well, they thought
They knew each other's dreams and hopes.
Themselves they questioned
And doubted.

How nice,
How nice they looked
To the public gaze which only glanced
At the figurines adorning the bench,
The decorations.

Right,
It was right
To sit and ask
Each other not
Themselves everything.

Perhaps,
Perhaps one day
The friends will learn
Of each other's existence
In the park of life.

GLENDA EVANS (student)

THE TRAVELLER

Old man, old man, sitting on the stile,
Your boots are worn, your clothes are torn,
    Tell us why you smile.

Children, children, what silly things you are!
My boots are worn and my clothes are torn
    Because I've walked so far.

Old man, old man, where have you walked from?
Your legs are bent, your breath is spent –
    Which way did you come?

Children, children, when you're old and lame,
When your legs are bent and your breath is spent
    You'll know the way I came.

Old man, old man, have you far to go
Without a friend to your journey's end,
    And why are you so slow?

Children, children, I do the best I may:
I meet a friend at my journey's end
    With whom you'll meet some day.

Old man, old man, sitting on the stile,
How do you know which way to go,
    And why is it you smile?

Children, children, butter should be spread,
Floors should be swept and promises kept –
    And you should be in bed!

RAYMOND WILSON

133

REACT

Consider the following questions in pairs, then share your findings with the whole class.

'THE TRAVELLER'

1 Although 'The Traveller' seems to be a simple poem, it uses all of these poetic devices:

- repetition   • verse pattern
- rhyme   • rhythm
- mood

Explore the use of each of these devices in the poem.

2 (a) What does the old man mean when he says, 'You'll know the way
        I came'?
   (b) Who is the old man's friend?
   (c) Did the old man actually answer the children's question 'How do you
        know which way to go?'
   (d) He certainly didn't directly answer the question 'And why is it you
        smile?' Why do *you* think the old man is smiling?

3 This poem could be read in two ways. On the one hand, it can be taken as
   the actual story of an old traveller at the end of a long journey. On the
   other hand, the traveller and the journey can be seen as metaphors for
   other things. What could they be?

'THE PARK BENCH'

This poem was written by a student of about your own age. In pairs, devise
your own set of comments and/or questions about 'The Park Bench' and
share them with the class. Usually, questions and comments will be about
what the poet is saying and how she is saying it. Make two lists:

Comments
- We really like ...
- ... is an unusual image

Questions
- What does the poet mean ...?
- When ...?
- Why ...?

'FARM CHILD'

In your pairs, answer YES or NO to each item in this checklist. To answer
the questions, you will need to explore and discuss the poem carefully. When
you have finished, compare your ideas with those of the rest of the class.
If you disagree on any items, give reasons for your particular decision in
each case.

Checklist

1 The farm boy has birds' nests stuffed under his hat.

2 Among other treasures in his pockets, the farm boy has some fruit.

3 The farm boy has a smallish face covered by a lot of unruly hair.

4 The poet clearly respects the young farm boy.

5 The poet suggests that nature responds to such natural, 'earthy' people.

6 'Look', 'mark' and 'notice' are probably the most important words
   in the poem.

RESPOND

1 Respond to one of these photographs by writing a reflective poem. Model your poem on one of the above three poems, if you like.

• What do you dream?

• Oodgeroo Noonuccal (Kath Walker)

or

2 'The Traveller' is the classic wise old man. If you know some wise old people, ask them for some words of wisdom. Arrange these in prose or poetry form.

or

3 There are quite a few poems which, like 'Farm Child', discuss the content of children's minds, dreams or imaginations. Describe what might be preoccupying *one* of these young people – or choose a character of your own if you wish:
- a computer addict
- a cricket fan
- a child who loves soldiers
- a car fanatic
- a musician
- a surf fanatic.

Write your results in prose or poetry. You might like to use words like 'look', 'mark' and 'notice', as the poet has done, to help structure your writing.

READ

Each of the following poems, written by students of about your own age, describes an imaginary 'escape' from the real world. Study each carefully and decide which you think is the better poem.

DREAMS

In an untamed
Corner of the park,
A newspaper flutters
In the breeze,
Sunning itself
In peaceful oblivion.
On the back page,
Next to the comics,
Above the Super Sunday
Crossword,
The advertisement
Shouts
'Let us Make
Your Wildest
Dreams Come True'.
A scrap is torn off
And freed, it floats away
Across the park.

'Dreams',
It says.
Just the one word,
'Dreams'.
Dreams,
Gliding
Unperturbed
Over the rubbish in the park;
Broken twigs,
Crumbling leaves,
Cigarette butts,
Empty wine bottles.

'Dreams',
Says the paper,
Skipping lightly
Over the rubbish,
Unsullied by what it passes.
Our dreams
Dance daintily over
The filthy truth
Of the world,
Borne by the
Breezes
Of life
And chance.

Our dreams
Know no limits,
Whirling around
As they journey
To wherever
They may go.
Strange, that a scrap
Of newspaper
Could mean so much;
The freedom of unchained
Imagination,
Winged unicorns,
Magic dragons,
Glorious light,
Happy endings,
Undying love.
The message
Holds me in its power,

Entranced,
Lost
In another world.
But now, without warning,
A little boy
Bursts my bubble.
Screaming through the park,
Shattering my peace,
He jumps on the paper,
Sinking it into the mud.
In a small brown puddle
The paper slowly drowns.
'Dreams' is swallowed
By filth.
Only a scrap
Of yesterday's paper.
Six letters.
A word.
No more.
Why then should I suddenly
Feel so sad?
As though the clumsy boy,
Not knowing, not caring,
Has smashed a magic palace
Made of
Nothing
But dreams.
'Dreams,' I mutter bitterly,
'Dreams.'

SAMANTHA CLARKE (student)

A MATHS LESSON

Four brick walls, and carpeted flooring,
An insistent buzzing of humanoid speech.
My mind wanders, allowing me to
Hear what I will.

By this act of wilful escapism
Each wall crumbles slowly,
The patches of sky increasing each second.
At last colour in unison.

Strangely, the floor washes away also,
Replaced by hot white sand.
The water laps, translucent but blue,
Startlingly real.

Lifting my spirits, washing my soul,
Relaxing and secure.
A seagull idly circles; and
Freedom is blue.

Something filters through the landscape,
The day's scenery slides away.
The seagull returns, asking me to
Define $E=mc2$.

This is when the walls reappear, and I
am left with my memories, confusingly familiar,
of dampness and sand in my shoes.
Brick walls are jail.

KATE WILKIN-SMITH (student)

REACT

Divide into two large groups – those who believe that 'Dreams' is the better
poem, and those who believe that 'A Maths Lesson' is the better poem.

Now conduct an informal debate. Members of each group must offer
comments and evidence to support their respective choice of poem. The side
which can offer the most support for their poem wins.

RESPOND

1   Write, in prose or poetry, a piece that begins with one of these lines or titles:

- In an untamed corner of my mind …
- Imagine …
- Lost in another world.
- Our dreams/Dance daintily over/The filthy truth/Of the world.
- Freedom is blue.

You may wish to brainstorm the possibilities of one or more of these titles as a whole class before you start your individual writing. Alternatively, your teacher may conduct a relaxation exercise or music session to allow you to *feel* the spirit of freedom and imagination.

or

2   Make a personal collage of 'dreams'. Use picture, prose and poetry snippets and anything else you think will work for you.

READ

These poems express yearning or desire. In each case the poet is so absorbed in this desire that he writes as if he is actually enjoying the longed-for experience.

SEA FEVER

I must down to the seas again, to the lonely sea and the sky,
And all I ask is a tall ship and a star to steer her by,
And the wheel's kick and the wind's song and the white sail's shaking,
And a grey mist on the sea's face and a grey dawn breaking.

I must down to the seas again, for the call of the running tide
Is a wild call and a clear call that may not be denied;
And all I ask is a windy day with the white clouds flying,
And the flung spray and the blown spume, and the seagulls crying.

I must down to the seas again, to the vagrant gypsy life,
To the gull's way and the whale's way where the wind's like a whetted knife;
And all I ask is a merry yarn from a laughing fellow-rover,
And quiet sleep and a sweet dream when the long trick's over.

JOHN MASEFIELD

THE DIVER

I would like to dive
Down
Into this still pool
Where the rocks at the bottom are safely deep,

Into the green
Of the water seen from within,
A strange light
Streaming past my eyes –

Things hostile,
You cannot stay here, they seem to say;
The rocks, slime-covered, the undulating
Fronds of weeds –

And drift slowly
Among the cooler zones;
Then, upward turning,
Break from the green glimmer

Into the light,
White and ordinary of the day,
And the mild air,
With the breeze and the comfortable shore.

W. W. E. ROSS

141

REACT
'THE DIVER'

1   What does the poet mean by these expressions?
    • the rocks are 'safely deep'
    • '... the undulating/Fronds of weeds –'
    • 'Into the light,/White and ordinary of the day,'
    • 'the comfortable shore'

2   The poet describes what the diver sees, in visual imagery. He also uses
    tactile imagery, images of touch and feeling, very subtly. 'Slime-covered'
    rocks for example, is a tactile image; the thought of how these rocks
    would feel probably strikes us more than the thought of how they
    would look.
    (a) Decide (as a class) which visual image is the most effective.
    (b) Find (as a class) all the tactile words – words that suggest touch or
    physical feeling.

3   Which lines particularly suggest that the poet has been well and truly carried away by his desire to dive into the pool?

'SEA FEVER'

The best way to appreciate this poem is to practise reading it aloud; its *sound* gives it its strength and its appeal. Here are some steps to help you. (See also reading guidelines on page v.)

1   Divide into three small groups. Each group is to explore, practise and present the poem orally to the rest of the class.

2   In each verse, note how the poet has used the following devices to achieve a rich sound effect:
    *   beautifully balanced lines in each stanza to create the poem's rhythm;
    *   alliteration ('a tall ship and a <u>s</u>tar to <u>s</u>teer her by'). When you emphasise alliterative words, you reinforce their sound effects;
    *   rhyming couplets (see **couplet**, page 146);
    *   repetition, which also strengthens the poem ('a wild call and a clear call').

3   In your groups, explore all of these features. Note and mark them where appropriate. It is a good idea, for example, to underline the alliteration so that you will remember to emphasise it.

142

4   In your groups, practise a choral reading of the poem.

5   When you have perfected your performance, present it to the other groups.

RESPOND

1   (a)   You are about to experience your first deep sea dive. In a paragraph of prose, capture the thoughts that race through your mind as you prepare to jump. Pay attention to your style of writing. Thoughts don't usually come in long, ordered sentences. Rather, they are often a muddle and clutter of single 'flashes' or ideas or rambling, disjointed words and phrases. If you use punctuation carefully, you should be able to achieve this effect.
       or
    (b)   Alternatively, describe – as the poet has done – the sights, sounds and feel of the underwater world. Write in prose or poetry – whichever you prefer.
       or

2   Write about your own sea fever in some way. You may have a love of swimming, surfing or sailing. Try to use some of the poetic devices used in the two poems: visual or tactile imagery, alliteration, rhyme and rhythm. (Remember that you can use poetic devices in prose as well as in poetry; they will make your writing richer and more effective.)
    or

3   Prepare and record a personal reading of 'The Diver'. See the poetry reading guidelines on page v before you start.

READ

These three poems express the poets' reflections on life and how it should be lived.

THE DOOR

Go and open the door.
    Maybe outside there's
    a tree, or a wood,
    a garden,
    or a magic city.

Go and open the door.
    Maybe a dog's rummaging.
    Maybe you'll see a face,
or an eye,
or the picture
            of a picture.

Go and open the door.
    If there's a fog
    it will clear.

Go and open the door.
Even if there's only
    the darkness ticking,
    even if there's only
    the hollow wind,
    even if
          nothing
              is there,
go and open the door.

At least
there'll be
a draught.

MIROSLAV HOLUB

143

ANTHEM FOR YOUTH

Why rush through our childhood,
To become the high and mighty adults
Whose calm authority hangs over us!
For we do not perceive their expressions
Of regret, as they realise just what
They sped through, not knowing their own happiness,
As their youth slipped away.

Why are we so eager to take on harsh responsibilities,
And leave our blissful innocence?
We dismiss the fun times – thinking only
Of our work, without noticing that
In 'Adult Life' there is no pocket money
For merely washing up.

MANDY FORD (student)

LEISURE

What is this life if, full of care,
We have no time to stand and stare?

No time to stand beneath the boughs
And stare as long as sheep or cows.

No time to see, when woods we pass,
Where squirrels hide their nuts in grass.

No time to see, in broad daylight,
Streams full of stars, like skies at night.

No time to turn at Beauty's glance,
And watch her feet, how they can dance.

No time to wait till her mouth can
Enrich that smile her eyes began.

A poor life this if, full of care,
We have no time to stand and stare.

WILLIAM H. DAVIES

REACT

Sit in one large circle as a whole class. Taking each poem one at a time, discuss:

1 The poem's theme or message. In other words, what is the poet saying about life or the way we should live it?

2 Discuss your reactions to each theme. Do you agree with the poet? Had you ever thought this way before?

To hold a successful 'circular discussion', all students should participate. To facilitate this, proceed around the circle clockwise. (There's always a volunteer who'll get things started!) Each student takes up the discussion where the preceding one finished. No-one should speak twice until all have had a say.

When you have exhausted discussion of one poem, proceed to the next. (If the circular response becomes a little tedious after the first poem, you may prefer to have an open, free discussion for a change.) Stay in your circle, however, as this really does inspire discussion and help communication.

RESPOND

1 Write the theme of each of these poems in the form of a commandment. Add to this to create your personal 'Commandments for Life and Living'. For example:
   • Thou shalt not be too eager to grow up (theme of 'Anthem for Youth' which was written by a student of about your age).
   or
2 Write your own poem about some aspect of life. You might like to use rhyming couplets (see **couplet**, page 146), as does the poem 'Leisure'. Start in a similar way: 'What is this life if...'.
   or
3 If you were inspired by 'The Door', write an essay about life's possibilities; about an imaginary adventure; about life beyond the 'prison' of your present existence. One of these titles may inspire you:
   • Beyond the door.
   • Maybe outside there's a ...
   • The darkness ticking.

145

GLOSSARY OF POETIC TERMS

alliteration This is the name given to the repeated use of the same sound at the beginning of two or more words that are close to each other. It helps the poet to create an effective sound, to emphasise certain words or to reinforce meaning.

aural imagery (See **image** below.) Aural imagery occurs when the poet uses words to appeal to our sense of hearing; words that suggest the sounds being made; for example: 'Bees are busy in the droning sky/The wind whistles, the pines sigh'.

ballad A story (or narrative) told in regular, rhyming, rhythmic stanzas. The first ballads were folk-poems or folk-songs, meant to be sung with musical accompaniment. They are simple, dramatic tales of events in human life and often have a chorus for communal presentation and participation.

couplet A couplet is a pair of rhyming lines. It is possible for a whole poem to be made up of couplets.

form This is the shape of a poem – the arrangement of words into lines and lines into verses or stanzas. This can be determined by the poet's use of rhyme and rhythm. If a poet chooses to write with a very regular rhyme and rhythm, the form is likely to be highly structured. (Compare with **free verse** below.)

free verse This is the name given to verse that does not have regular rhymes or rhythms or a formal or traditional stanza pattern. Nevertheless, it will have some informal rhyme and rhythm and its form or shape is deliberate and meaningful.

image A picture created with rich and evocative words. There are several types of images, of which visual images, aural images and tactile images are the most common (see above and page 147).

irony Irony occurs when the writer says one thing but clearly believes the opposite of what he says. It is a form of sarcasm; a 'tongue-in-cheek' way of saying something in order to ridicule or condemn it.

metaphor   When a poet speaks about something as though it were something else, we say the poet is using a metaphor. In 'Letter from Lilliput', for example (on page 55), the poet refers to cars as 'cocoons' and 'fish tanks'; these are metaphors. They help us to imagine or visualise what the poet has in mind. A metaphor is a special kind of image as it uses specially chosen words to help us picture what the poet is saying.

mood   The 'atmosphere' of a poem. Writers can create a particular mood or atmosphere by carefully choosing words and rhythms to suit the message of the poem, be it happy, sad, reverent or whatever.

personification   When a poet refers to an animal or an inanimate object as *if* it were a *person*, with human attributes, we call this '*person-if*ication'.

rhyme   When words at the *ends* of lines finish with the same sound, this is called 'end rhyme'. It is the most common rhyme in poetry. When words *within* the same line have matching sounds, this is called 'internal rhyme'.

simile   A simile is a poetic comparison: one thing is said to be like or similar to another. The word 'like' or 'as' usually appears in a simile. A simile is a specific image as it uses specially chosen words to help the reader picture what the poet is saying.

tactile imagery   (See **image** above.) Tactile imagery occurs when the poet uses words that appeal to our sense of touch; words that suggest how something might feel: 'slinky, slimey, slithery toads creep and crawl in the twitching night'.

theme   The topic or issue with which the poem is concerned. The theme is usually the idea or attitude that the poet wishes to communicate through his writing.

tone   This is similar to mood; it is the way the poem sounds to you, the impression you get of the poet's 'voice'. A tone may be angry, bitter, apologetic, reflective, sad, and so on. The poem's rhythm and language create its tone and thus suggest how it should be read.

visual image   A visual image is an image (see page 146) that appeals to our sense of sight. The poet uses tangible, descriptive words which help us to visualise what he or she is depicting.

147

ACKNOWLEDGEMENTS

Poetry and Extracts

Angus and Robertson Publishers for 'Legend' from *Collected Poems* by Judith Wright; Anvil Press Poetry Ltd for 'This England' by E A Markham from *E A Markham: Towards the End of a Century* published in 1989; Peter Appleton for 'The Responsibility'; Duncan Ball for 'Small Talk'; Anne Bell for 'The Kestrel'; Gyles Brandreth for 'Ode to a Goldfish' from *A Second Poetry Book* ed. John Foster published by Oxford University Press; The Calder Educational Trust, London for 'Revolver' by Alan Riddell from his volume *Eclipse* published by Calder and Boyars, London © Alan Riddell 1972; Carcanet Press Ltd for 'Archives' from *Poem Archives* by Edwin Morgan; Chatto and Windus for 'The Postman' from *Root and Branch* by Jon Stallworthy; Samantha Leigh Clarke for 'Dreams'; Collins/Angus and Robertson for 'Mulga Bill's Bicycle' and 'The Man from Ironbark' from *Collected Verse* by A B Paterson; The Estate of Stanley Cook for 'The Spider' © Stanley Cook from *A Second Poetry Book* ed. John Foster published by Oxford University Press; Dobson Books Ltd for 'Bronze and Silver' from *Good Company* by Leonard Clark published by Dobson Books Ltd; John Fairfax for 'Sonnet' from *100 Poems* published by Phoenix Press; Harcourt Brace Jovanovich Inc. for 'Worms in the Wind' from *Complete Poems* by Carl Sandburg and 'Yarns' from *The People, Yes* by Carl Sandburg; HarperCollins Publishers Ltd for 'Whisper Whisper' from *Rabbiting On And Other Poems* by Kit Wright published by Fontana Lions; David Higham Associates for 'Timothy Winters' from *Collected Poems* by Charles Causley; Hodder and Stoughton Ltd for 'If Words Were Birds', 'Daily London Recipe', 'I Am On The Kids' Side', and 'The Appeal' from *Up to Date* by Steve Turner; and for 'Night' from *Tapestry* by Eric Williams published by Edward Arnold; John Johnson Ltd for 'Warning' by Jenny Joseph from *Selected Poems* published by Bloodaxe Books Ltd © Jenny Joseph 1992. Larraine Kikkert for 'Reflections'; James Kirkup for 'The Caged Bird in Springtime"; Wes Magee for 'Sunday Morning' by Wes Magee from *Morning Break and Other Poems* by Wes Magee, published by Cambridge University Press 1989; Kate Wilkin-Smith for 'A Maths Lesson'; Spike Milligan Productions Ltd for 'Bad Report' from *Unspun Socks in a Children's Laundry* published by Michael Joseph Ltd; The National Exhibition of Children's Art for 'Anthem for Youth' by Mandy Ford from *Cadbury's Fourth Book of Children's Poetry*; Leslie Norris for 'The Ballad of Billy Rose' by Leslie Norris from *Rising Early* ed. Charles Causley; Oxford University Press for 'Emus' © Chris Wallace-Crabbe 1985 from *The Amorous Cannibal* by Chris Wallace-Crabbe 1985, for 'Out of School' © Hal Summers 1978 from *Tomorrow is My Love* by Hal Summers 1978;

148

Lydia Pender for 'The Ball' from *The Morning Magpie*; Penguin Books Ltd for 'The Door' from *Selected Poems* by Miroslav Holub, translated by Ian Milner and George Theiner Penguin Books 1967 © Miroslav Holub 1967, translation © Penguin Books Ltd 1967, and for 'Hair' by Max Fatchen from *Songs For My Dog and Other People* © Max Fatchen 1980 published by Viking Kestrel and in Puffin Books; Peters Fraser and Dunlop Group Ltd for 'The Big Baboon' from *Complete Verse* by Hilaire Belloc and for 'Happiness' from *Gig* and 'Smithereen' from *In the Glassroom* and for 'Fifteen Million Plastic Bags' by Adrian Mitchell from *For Beauty Douglas* (Neither this nor any other of Adrian Mitchell's poems is to be used in connection with any examination whatsoever.) and for 'Estate', 'Mad Ad', 'The First Day at School', 'The Commission' from *In the Glassroom* by Roger McGough and 'Bradford' from *Gig* by Roger McGough; Murray Pollinger Literary Agent for 'The Centipede Song' from *James and the Giant Peach* by Roald Dahl published by Penguin Books Ltd; James Reeves' Estate for 'Miss Wing' and 'Cows' © James Reeves from *The Wandering Moon and Other Poems* (Puffin Books) by James Reeves; Rogers, Coleridge and White Ltd for 'It's Poisoning Down' from *Thawing Frozen Dogs* by Brian Patten published by Viking; Suzanne Rogers for 'Pier'; Kate Stevenson for 'A Lost Dreamtime'; Colin Thiele for 'Tom Farley'; R S Thomas for 'Farm Child' © R S Thomas; University Press of New England for 'Counting the Mad' by Donald Justice from *The Summer Anniversaries, Revised Edition* © 1981 Donald Justice, Wesleyan University Press; University of Queensland Press for 'Evening' from *The Other Side of the Fence* by Peter Kocan 1975; Vernon Watkins for 'Midnight' from *The Ballad of the Mari Lwyd*; A P Watt Ltd on behalf of The Trustees of the Robert Graves Copyright Trust for 'A Frosty Night' published in *Collected Poems 1975* by Robert Graves; Colin West for 'A Wisp of a Wasp' from *The Best of the West* c Colin West 1992; John Updike for 'Mirror' © John Updike 1957 from *The Carpentered Hen and Other Tame Creatures* by permission of Alfred A Knopf Inc. Originally appeared in *The New Yorker*.

149

Photos and Cartoons

Allsport UK p93 middle; Bettman Archives p93 top; Coo-ee Picture Library p93 bottom; © London Express News and Feature Service p4; © Creator's Syndicate Cartoon p6; Sara McMillan p135 top; News Limited pp68, 93 centre, 100 bottom right and top, 105 right and left, 119, 135 bottom; Reuters pp92, 100 bottom left.

Disclaimer

INDEX OF POETS

INDEX OF TITLES
AND FIRST LINES

153